PRAISE FOR *AFTER T...*

After the Adults Change is a manifesto
ticularly relevant at a time when societ
and role of schools in delivering more than simply academic education.

PHIL NAYLOR, PODCAST HOST, *NAYLOR'S NATTER*, DEPUTY HEAD TEACHER AND LOCAL AUTHORITY GOVERNOR

After the Adults Change has something for everyone. It isn't just about supporting the children who bring behavioural challenges; it also has practical ideas and advice and recognises the needs of those children who just want to learn.

SHARON PASCOE, HEAD TEACHER, FOCHRIW PRIMARY SCHOOL AND BRYN AWEL PRIMARY SCHOOL

Paul Dix provides a straight-talking practical blueprint to help schools create a positive and constructive culture around behaviour and relationships. Paul's wealth of experience makes *After the Adults Change* a modern classic and a book of the times that is an essential read for all school leaders.

JON TAIT, DEPUTY CEO AND DIRECTOR OF SCHOOL IMPROVEMENT, ARETÉ LEARNING TRUST

Paul Dix is amazing! His writing is full of warmth and sincerity, and his care for teachers and students shines through in his latest offering. In our post-COVID-19 world, teachers and educators need to keep supporting our kids through these turbulent times – and *After the Adults Change* shows us how it can be done!

KARL C. PUPÉ, TEACHER, FOUNDER OF ACTIONHEROTEACHER.COM,
AND AUTHOR OF *THE ACTION HERO TEACHER: CLASSROOM MANAGEMENT MADE SIMPLE*

After the Adults Change is written with a kindness and sensitivity that mirrors exactly the tone that a classroom or school built on 'ready, respectful and safe' would have. It is a positive, supportive and considered work that provides numerous reminders of why we do what we do along with strategies and suggestions, genuine examples of these in practice, and the characteristic, self-deprecating humour that made *When the Adults Change, Everything Changes* such an accessible and yet powerful read.

COLIN GOFFIN, DIRECTOR OF EDUCATION, BIG PICTURE LEARNING UK

If you want to transform the way that your school community 'does behaviour', then *After the Adults Change* is the book for you. Paul's strong belief, based on real-life research and practice, that the culture of a school is a reflection of the behaviour and attitude of the adults is compelling and truly inspirational.

MARC DOYLE, DIRECTOR OF EDUCATION, CONSILIUM ACADEMIES, AND EXPERIENCED HEAD TEACHER

After the Adults Change is a refreshing, intelligent, thought-provoking and easy-to-read book. I love the layout and how Paul uses evidence based theory and real-life case studies to support his writing. The book contains many new heart-centred approaches and takeaways to put into practice, especially at the end of each chapter in the 'Stop that!', 'How to lead it' and 'Nuggets' sections. I could, in fact, write a book about this book; however, I will stop and allow you to read and digest this ground-breaking book for yourself.

LAURA HENRY-ALLAIN, MBE, AWARD-WINNING GLOBAL WRITER, SPEAKER AND CONSULTANT

This book is about sustained, achievable, long-term school improvement. The behaviour nirvana is characterised by an embedded whole school culture of high expectations, the development of skilled and reflective professional practitioners, and high levels of pupil agency.

SIMON KIDWELL, HEAD TEACHER, HARTFORD MANOR PRIMARY SCHOOL AND NURSERY

All children deserve to feel safe, loved and valued – and if this is your mantra, then grab this book with both hands and enjoy the read. From behaviour management strategy to everyday practical tips, there is something for everyone in *After the Adults Change*. Here's to continuing the revolution and ensuring that school years lead to a bright future of choice and opportunity for all.

KATIE ROBERTS, HEAD TEACHER, DA VINCI ACADEMY

After the Adults Change is the perfect guide to strengthening relationships with children and young people and to ensuring positive behaviour, from both children and adults. This book should be your companion to introducing and embedding relational approaches, whether on a class or whole school level. It is a hugely practical resource for every adult who works with children and young people.

JENNIFER M. KNUSSEN, HEAD TEACHER, PITTEUCHAR EAST PRIMARY SCHOOL AND NURSERY

AFTER THE
ADULTS
CHANGE

ACHIEVABLE
BEHAVIOUR
NIRVANA

PAUL DIX

independent
thinking press

First published by

Independent Thinking Press
Crown Buildings, Bancyfelin, Carmarthen, Wales, SA33 5ND, UK
www.independentthinkingpress.com
and
Independent Thinking Press
PO Box 2223, Williston, VT 05495, USA
www.crownhousepublishing.com

Independent Thinking Press is an imprint of Crown House Publishing Ltd.

© Paul Dix, 2021

The right of Paul Dix to be identified as the author of this work
has been asserted by him in accordance with the Copyright,
Designs and Patents Act 1988.

Illustration © David Bull, 2021

David Bull has asserted his right under the Copyright, Designs and
Patents Act 1988, to be identified as the illustrator of this work.

First published 2021.

Quotes from Government documents used in this publication have been approved under an Open
Government Licence. Please visit www.nationalarchives.gov.uk/doc/open-government-licence/.

All rights reserved. Except as permitted under current legislation no part of this work may be
photocopied, stored in a retrieval system, published, performed in public, adapted, broadcast,
transmitted, recorded or reproduced in any form or by any means, without the prior permission of
the copyright owners. Enquiries should be addressed to Independent Thinking Press.

Independent Thinking Press has no responsibility for the persistence or accuracy of URLs for
external or third-party websites referred to in this publication, and does not guarantee that any
content on such websites is, or will remain, accurate or appropriate.

Edited by Ian Gilbert

British Library Cataloguing-in-Publication Data
A catalogue entry for this book is available from the British Library.

Print ISBN 978-178135377-6
Mobi ISBN 978-178135392-9
ePub ISBN 978-178135393-6
ePDF ISBN 978-178135394-3

LCCN 2021932299

Printed and bound in the UK by
Gomer Press, Llandysul, Ceredigion

DEDICATION

My Granny was Austrian and she made the best *vanillekipferl* anyone has ever eaten. Don't @ me with your recipes – I am not prepared to argue about that. She was gentle and kind with a strong Austrian accent that she tried to hide from years of having to. Mitsy, as she was known, had escaped the Jewish ghettos just before the Second World War, sponsored by an Englishman to work as a domestic servant in a large country house. She was a refugee who left her sisters and family behind to grab a chance of a safer life. That story is remarkable enough. Being an Austrian woman in England in 1938 and living without being able to speak English rendered her voiceless. Yet she had a voice stronger than we ever knew and a story that was only revealed to me recently.

In 1937, at the age of 25, she wrote an article that was published in a German newspaper. That is a remarkable feat for a woman so young. The article was heavily and openly critical of Hitler. She did not hold back. Mitsy was subsequently arrested and spent a year in prison. A true heroine, she never spoke to anyone about it. We are still uncovering the details.

I know that it is right to speak out against injustice, even in the face of those who seek to muddle the truth. Maybe strength is inherited, not created. So, this book is for you, Maria Hedwig Greimann, who, in the face of immediate risk to her own life and liberty, spoke truth to power. I hope I have even an ounce of her courage, humility and strength. I won't hold back either.

CONTENTS

INTRODUCTION

There is a behavioural nirvana. One that is calm, purposeful and respectful, where poor behaviour is as rare as a PE teacher in trousers and relationships drive achievement. Annoyingly, and predictably, the road is hard and the ride bumpy and littered with clichés. It is achievable, though, and when you get there it is a little slice of relational heaven.

The steps outlined in *When the Adults Change, Everything Changes* are about shifting the behaviour of the adults and changing the response the child receives.[1] You will soak that up through this book too. Read them in any order – the core message is the same. Your deliberate calm, consistent and planned behaviour underpins everything.

If you are anything like me, you can read a book, take away three useful things and then move on. If you have read and implemented *When the Adults Change, Everything Changes* like a legend then get ticking. If not, here is a quick reminder of the foundations of the approach – the five pillars of practice.

1. Consistent, calm adult behaviour.

   ● Don't shout or respond emotionally to poor behaviour.

   ● Responses are always rational and planned.

   ● Adult behaviour is deliberately modified to make the team effort consistent.

   ● Your model of being a rounded human being does a lot of the heavy lifting.

---

1   Paul Dix, *When the Adults Change, Everything Changes: Seismic Shifts in School Behaviour* (Carmarthen: Independent Thinking Press, 2017).

2. First attention for best conduct.

- You will get more of the behaviour you notice the most.
- School culture shifts when the focus shifts to the 95% of children who come every day, who do the right thing, who are honest, disciplined and diligent.
- Recognition mechanisms are used in every lesson to acknowledge effort, not achievement.
- Positive notes, positive phone calls and Hot Chocolate Friday are huge wins for minimal effort.

3. Relentless routines.

- Meet and greet at the door of every classroom and position non-teaching colleagues strategically throughout the school.
- The rules are limited to three words: ready, respectful, safe.
- Deliberate teacher routines are designed to make transitions easy for everyone (e.g. calling the class to silence, signals for the start of a task/end of a lesson, transition rituals).

4. Scripting difficult interventions.

- Interventions are designed so that staff can hold the boundaries while staying calm.
- Rational steps to address poor behaviour include scripted interventions and planned conversations.
- Consistent use of the 30 second intervention script by all adults.

5. Restorative follow-up.

- Restorative conversations are chosen for incidents that need restoration.
- Relational paths out of difficult events are preferred to punishment roads.
- Students get what they need, not just what they deserve.

After the adults have changed, there is an opportunity to go faster, wider and deeper. To embed positive classroom cultures soaked in humble recognition, to cast a critical eye over the use of proportionate consequences, to further refine support for children who struggle with it all and to map out a route for radical, sustained behaviour improvement.

This book will challenge you to rejig your time to introduce coaching for every child and refresh your restorative approach to keep everyone thinking. We will look at the knotty issues that need to be overcome when holding to inclusive values and explore how to lead your classroom or school like a plodding tortoise, not a performance enhanced hare. We will look in detail at how to support those who cause chaos while protecting those who just want to learn. And we will do it all without blame or any notion that a child's behaviour is the fault of the teacher.

I will share work that I am inspired by, including the Glasgow Model (and from schools across Scotland) which has reduced exclusion and improved provision for those at the margins. We will drop in and learn from schools who have been 'Paul Dixing it'[2] for years and those who are innovating brilliantly with the strategies from the start. Along the way, I will reaffirm my commitment to managing behaviour with calm humility and the right of every child to learn in peace – and my utter disdain for ludicrous notions of zero tolerance/no excuses and any other euphemism for being shitty to kids.

People, strap in, tables in the upright position, one hand on the oxygen mask and let's go.

---

2   A terrifying phrase apparently in common usage in Scottish schools. I am sure it is also to be heard with accompanying swearing.

Chapter 1

EMOTIONALLY CONSISTENT TEACHING

Calm, predictable, safe.

A deliberate tightening of consistency, which was central to *When the Adults Change, Everything Changes*, often achieves great leaps in improved behaviour. The essential daily drumbeat of the same rules, calm, smiling adults and predictable responses lay the foundations for a climate that works for everyone. When the adults change, everything changes is the first principle, so your behaviour is an important focus. As the revolution in practice begins to normalise, you will need to be ready to adapt your own behaviour further. You are no longer standing on the barricades persuading your colleagues to change, but don't lower that flag just yet, soldier. There is work to be done.

Once you have upgraded your own professional behaviour and relationships, there are further consistencies that will make your classroom a safer, more predictable and better place to learn. I know that your ability to suppress the natural emotional responses to poor behaviour is now well rehearsed and practised. I am sure you have perfected the poker face and can control your rolling eyes, screwface or twitchy blink like a mannequin. Legend. In your mind you have separated forever the child's negative emotional response from your own. You have become curious about distressed children, not angry with naughty scrotes. You recognise secondary behaviour when it is thrown at you and you know there is a better time and place to respond to it. When you look back at your worst moments, you laugh at your own ridiculousness. There is now a different level of emotional control that pervades every interaction. Zen-like, you float between incidents. Your inner peace (or at least your 'pretending to be at peace') means that you can start to see through the behaviour to what is being communicated.

It takes time to find the balance between being your true self and being the person your pupils need. The two are rarely the same. Context also matters. Being transparent, open and honest with some classes is a fast track to relational currency. With others, it means getting mugged off and asked by every giggling child you meet for the next six months, 'Sir, is your middle name really Susan?' Revealing too much of yourself too soon is a crapshoot. It might go brilliantly, but in all probability you will end up rolling a 7, walking home in the rain and wishing you had never picked up the dice.

When you have been at a school for some time, you may allow yourself a slightly smug smile when you hear of another new teacher explaining that they told the class about their slam poetry YouTube channel. 'You told them *what?!*' is always funny because we have all trodden much the same route. I wanted so desperately to be the teacher I never had that I thought I could mimic the performance of a great teacher, but behind that performance there was no substance. Being an emotionally consistent adult takes most of us a long time. We get better incrementally, not in one dramatic leap.

EMOTIONAL CONSISTENCY AND REFINING ROUTINES

Visible and audible consistencies make the school live and breathe with your values. Emotional consistencies are harder to pin down but no less critical. Emotional consistency for the children comes with the ability of the adults to control their emotions in response to poor behaviour, and instead put empathy and logic at the heart of each interaction. Easy to say, hard to do on a Thursday afternoon when you have been run ragged by Chelsea and her attempts to gradually and discreetly complete a full facial over the course of three lessons. Unregulated children need obviously regulated adults, even if their behaviour seems designed to frustrate this.

Predictability makes classrooms feel safe. Routines are central to this predictability. In lessons, refining the routines so they can be triggered quickly and executed deftly is a driver of productivity.

I recently watched a teacher working with a class of 8- and 9-year-olds and was struck on entering the room that some of the children were proudly wearing golden, sparkly top hats. In fact, they seemed to walk a little taller in the hat – it bestowed a certain authority and swagger. Like a PE teacher with a new clipboard.

The hats were 'golden peer assessment hats' (I know, dangerously progressive) and were used to recognise the 'assessor'. The pleasure on the children's faces when wearing and then passing on the hat to another child was wonderful to behold. They were having a whale of a time, yet the class were focused, disciplined and caught up in the learning. The transitions in the activity were effortless: the hat was passed and the roles changed.

What was perhaps even more impressive was the transition to a new activity. The teacher's count was just a quiet 'Three, two, one.' The hats disappeared in an instant and they were ready for the next part of the lesson. This seemingly effortless transition demonstrated how determined the teacher was to get her classroom running like clockwork. She was never going to be satisfied with routines that were just OK. Her high standards and expectations for routines translated into a very productive classroom, but they were also a model for the children and promoted a safe environment. The climate was set. With these mechanics in place, everyone worked more efficiently to squeeze a little extra out of every lesson. Everyone felt safer inside the predictable roles and rituals.

Without refined routines there is too much improvisation, too much surprise and too much chance of some children losing their way, day after day. Around the site, the sharper the routines, the greater the predictability and sense of security. In many schools, fantastic walking (hands behind the back, chest out, walking with purpose – and an idea originally created by Margaret Farrell) has fast become wonderful walking. Young children particularly love it. It isn't really a strategy for a secondary school, although with tongue in cheek I would have a go. Fantastic walking has also given birth to a series of alliterative offspring including legendary line-ups, spectacular silence, marvellous moving (where not all the children can walk) and perhaps, in some far off mutation, quintessential queuing. The same principles are at work.

There is a world of difference between teaching positive routines using gentle reinforcement that the pupils enjoy and drilling children with micromanaged compliance routines. Some authoritarians pursue 'do as you are told' routines and pretend they are quite reasonable. Compliance routines – standing up when an adult walks in, fingers on lips, look at me when I am talking to you, track the speaker and so on – are more about exerting authority and control than improving teaching and learning. They chill the climate in the classroom. In these schools, relational practice is considered less important than power. Nobody is truly happy learning in such a culture.

CHOPPER HARRIS

Mr 'Chopper' Harris, my teacher for many years, was an expert in quashing any notion of a positive relationship. Chopper became a teacher after leaving the navy. He was called Chopper, as legend had it, because he shot off his own thumb with his rifle. Quite how you achieve that I have still not been able to work out.

He was a uniquely strange and oft-times violent man with a dry sense of humour. Chopper was incredible and terrifying all at once. His opening ritual for the lesson was to slowly, dramatically, tilt his head backwards and spread his handkerchief over his face, cleaning his glasses and blowing his nose in one ridiculous but oddly mesmeric action. He would then lay out the pages of *Sporting Life* (a sports newspaper best known for its coverage of horse racing) across his desk, carefully turning each page by pinching the top right corner, and set about choosing the horses he would bet on while we got on with page 12, exercise 4.

At lunchtime he would visit the betting shop and boozer that were conveniently situated next door to each other. If you had him after lunch, and the bets hadn't gone his way, the board rubber was thrown with increasingly aggressive abandon. Once, memorably, his aim was blunted by a couple of extra whiskeys and the board rubber smashed the window and ended up on the street outside. He commanded me to go and pick it up so he could throw it at me again. Children would regularly get injured by mahogany board rubbers and not think it worth a mention. 'Oh that [touches gaping head wound], just had Chopper.' 'Oh right.'

It is safe to say that I struggled to learn much at all in his lessons, so fascinated was I by Chopper's idiosyncrasies and propensity for rough justice. I lived in a perpetual state of fear that I would be the next recipient of board rubber justice and excitement that it might be someone else. You never quite knew where you were with Chopper. This was deliberate. Chopper was not a teacher ever in pursuit of relationships with his charges. He was not a man with empathy. At least, not at work.

When teaching, Chopper had four levels of emotion which were triggered by four key phrases delivered in a voice as deep and gruff as you can imagine. 'Pipe down' was level one – a general plea to the assembled teenagers that he wanted their attention. It was expressed almost casually, as if he knew it would be ignored. With an increase in volume and a sense of urgency, 'Will you pipe down' signalled a shift in his degree of frustration. The third and fourth levels were often indistinguishable. There was certainly no gap between the final, 'WOULD YOU KINDLY PLEASE PIPE DOWN' and the throwing of the hardwood (polished daily) blackboard rubber at the head of some unsuspecting young miscreant. The terror was at times amusing, often bruising, occasionally terrifying.

I am sure that you are not in the habit of shouting at children or throwing objects at them to make your point. However, you may have your own levels of frustration that trigger and accelerate your own emotions. Just check the next time you get annoyed: how 'playable' are you?

THE UNPROVOKABLE ADULT

Adults like Chopper, who wear their heart on their sleeve, create an anxious climate. They undermine the emotional security they should be nurturing. The direct connection between the child's behaviour and the emotional state of the adult is obvious. Some children will immediately recognise the emotional state, empathise with it and change their behaviour. After all, they are able to accurately identify negative emotions and respond accordingly. Some children. Not mine. Not many. The obvious temptation for any child is to see how they can provoke that emotion. To test that the link between their behaviour and the adult response is still there. To find out just how playable the adults are.

'Joel, stop swinging in the chair. It's annoying me.'

'Emile, that tapping is driving me crazy.'

'Jasmin, if you interrupt me one more time I'm going to explode!'

There may be a time, when trust has developed, for wearing your heart on your sleeve, but in the early days with a new class you might want to hide your heart up your jumper. There are better ways to build great relationships.

Attending a speed awareness course recently provoked the same temptation in me to play with the 'adults'. Interestingly, the vigorous bonhomie and jovial style came to an abrupt halt when I dared to ask a difficult question. The course facilitators threatened me with exclusion from the room. Apparently, the booths at the Holiday Inn are for a different purpose. However, I was saved, beautifully, by the appearance of a latecomer who burst in, sat down and promptly fell asleep and started snoring. They didn't like that at all.

If you lay out a buffet of adult emotions, don't be surprised if some children want to try everything on the table. The connection between your emotion and their poor behaviour is one that you need to break. Instead, make the connection between their behaviour and the standards you expect in your lesson. Your behaviour → my emotion → emotionally fuelled punishment is a common chain of events. The change comes when you remove your emotion every time: your behaviour → our rules/standards/agreements → proportionate response.

What children really need is an unprovokable adult, especially one who lives with adults not afraid of losing their temper. An emotionally predictable learning environment is one where the negative emotion of the adults is all but absent. When you are talking to children about their behaviour, even in the calmest moments, be careful not to reinforce the connection accidentally.

'Now, you know that I can't stand it when …'

'That noise really irritates me …'

'The next person who shouts out/stands up/stage dives will not see another breaktime before adulthood!'

There must be no chance of the children controlling the adults. If you give children a route map of your emotions, you are giving them the opportunity to take control away from you at a moment's notice. Any climate adjustment must be your planned decision, not shifted by remote control by a bored child.

NURTURE FROM THE FIRST STEP

Nurture starts at the school gate and the classroom door, but shaking hands with students now feels like a tale from the old country. The COVID-19 interruption to our lives, and the physical distancing that has accompanied it, means things have changed. In recent times, you would be more likely to run a successful CPD session on Thinking Hats than you would to shake hands with every child. What was formerly a great way to meet and greet will now be a safeguarding concern.

We may need to adapt them for our socially distanced times, but the principles of meet and greet still apply. The connection may not be physical – no more handshakes, fist bumps or high fives – but we can still have fun:

- Air high five
- Bowing graciously
- Cheesy double thumbs-up
- Elbow bump
- Foot tap
- Hand on heart 'shake'
- Namaste
- Salute

- Sign language 'Good morning'

- Special dance

- Wave

Or just smile. Door signs can seem gimmicky but they are so much more than that. They give children control over how to engage, relieving anxiety and making the interaction safe on their terms. Likewise, the videos that many teachers have posted on social media of children meeting and greeting their teachers seem schmaltzy but the children love them. They give some students something to look forward to in the morning. Accept that on some days you won't feel like it, but for many young people it is the only positive adult greeting they ever get.

Interestingly, meet and greet is a common intervention across very different schools. More traditional environments love it because it creates a formality and politeness that is a strong model for adult life. It fits well into silent corridors, the teacher as an authority figure and linear behaviour policies. More progressive schools love it because it connects adults and students ready for a collaborative approach to learning. It is where the roads meet: an essential part of very different school cultures and ways of managing behaviour and relationships.[1]

---

1   For more on this, see: Clayton R. Cook, Aria Fiat, Madeline Larson, Christopher Daikos, Tal Slemrod, Elizabeth A. Holland, Andrew J. Thayer and Tyler Renshaw, Positive Greetings at the Door: Evaluation of a Low-Cost, High-Yield Proactive Classroom Management Strategy, *Journal of Positive Behavior Interventions*, 20(3) (2018): 149–159. In his summary of the study, Youki Terada concludes that welcoming students 'sets a positive tone and can increase engagement and reduce disruptive behavior'. The social and emotional support 'promotes a sense of belonging' and 'helps them feel invested in their learning'. Furthermore, engagement increased by 20% and disruptive behaviour decreased by 9%: Youki Terada, Welcoming Students with a Smile, *Edutopia* (11 September 2018). Available at: https://www.edutopia.org/article/welcoming-students-smile.

The quickest way to kill enthusiasm for meeting and greeting at the door is to force adults to greet children in a certain way. No grown-up needs that level of micromanagement. The point of the meet and greet is to make the children feel safe, not to make the adults feel awkward. I love the embellished greetings and creative energy that has emerged, but it is important to remain authentic. If a high five doesn't work for you and you are comfortable with simply saying hello at the door, then you should do just that. Children sniff out a fake very quickly. Letting meet and greet be more natural might allow everyone to relax and bring in those who were reluctant to 'perform' at the height of the behaviour revolution.

The problem of expecting all children to shake hands was effortlessly dissipated by Newtongrange Primary School in Dalkeith, Scotland, with their classroom door checklists. Nobody is forced to do anything they are not entirely comfortable with and the children choose how they will meet and greet their teacher.

On a visit to Newtongrange Primary School, I saw not only how far they had come in transforming behaviour, but I also, finally, achieved the status one can only dream of. The teacher welcomed me into the classroom like an old friend, and I was surprised that when introduced to the class they seemed to recognise my name. Not with the usual giggles that naturally accompany the announcement of my surname; no, this time with a mutter of appreciation. I thought it was odd for thirty 9-year-old children in Scotland to know my name. These weren't my, ahem, 'Endz'. The teacher then revealed that the class had recently been put into reading groups which they had named after significant authors: Burns, Shakespeare, Dickens and Dix. (OK, so I am not at all sure of the other three, but when I heard my own name I forgot everything else!) I still don't think the teacher realises just how proud I am of appearing in that surreal line-up.

LACEYFIELD: A HIVE OF RESTORATIVE PRACTICE

When Emma Beveridge arrived at LaceyField (the home of Eastfield Infants' and Nursery Academy and Lacey Gardens Junior Academy) as executive principal, the school had the highest rate of fixed-term exclusion of any school within the trust. In Louth, a relatively isolated market town, the school serves a deprived community with a high level of pupil premium children. The sanction led approach to managing behaviour was not serving the children, the staff or the community.

Emma and the LaceyField team flipped the school from reliance on fixed-term exclusions and lesson removal to trauma informed, relational practice and calm, consistent adults. The school's emphasis on a team approach meant that she was able to take all of her colleagues with her.

At LaceyField, the children's excellent conduct is recognised using the Bees. The mission, created by the staff, is to be *busy being brilliant*. The children are recognised for using their bee-haviours for learning: be brave, be kind, be in charge of me, be grateful, be curious, be on the team. They have Bees for learning, Bees for being brave and Bees for being brilliant. Recognition boards are buzzing with Bees! And there are hives of recognition all over the school. Adults use positive postcards and positive phone calls home to drive a culture that is dripping with recognition for those children going over and above.

Relationships are at the heart of all they do. The school starts each day with a nurture breakfast and the children work in 'Kingdoms' which are made up of three classes. The family team of learning means that the children feel safe, supported and connected.

The ethos at LaceyField is one of 'done with' rather than 'done to'. They have worked with restorative legend Mark Finnis to shape their restorative practice. The leadership team believe in a ripple effect: if they are well in themselves and act with kindness and love, that will ripple out to the staff, and that in turn will ripple out to the children and their families. It is what they truly believe and why their restorative ethos is so strong.

There is a dedicated care team which organises support for children who are struggling. At LaceyField, they seek to understand each child and meet them where they are. They know that relationships make the difference and use their understanding of the Neurosequential

Model of Therapeutics to support children's emotional, social and mental health development.

They work on the 'name it to tame it' approach to emotional intelligence so that conversations about emotions are explicit. Children are supported to recognise and control their emotions. Self-regulation is taught deliberately and not left to chance. They also use sensory circuits where children engage in physical regulation activities – for example, using a yoga ball to apply pressure to a child's back (like a massage). They call it 'Squash'!

Emma refers to LaceyField as a 'brick mother': 'The culture is the foundation, and curriculum and pedagogy are the bricks and mortar. At LaceyField, we have a positive approach to behaviour relationships and life. We focus on the class as a family team and quality first teaching.'

THE OTHER ADULTS IN THE ROOM

Your introduction to a new class of children will inevitably also be an introduction to other adults who may spend all or some of their time in your lessons. Leaving them as an afterthought is not just rude, it is missing a trick. Another adult might complicate or unintentionally upset the emotional consistency in your lesson if agreements aren't made and monitored.

If you involve them in your thinking and your plan for managing behaviour and relationships, if you give them equal status in the room, then teamwork becomes natural – like two parents (without the sniping, plate-throwing and sleeping in the shed). There are some quick wins here. Spend time going through your behaviour plan with the adults who regularly work alongside you. It will be time worth investing.

You might want to start with the classroom plan or with the values that sit behind it. The small stuff is important here: the tighter you are in the planning, the closer you will appear to be in front of the children. The parts of the plan that can go wrong easily when two people are trying to work in tandem need to be discussed. You will need to return to these at the end of every day until you are both in the same groove.

Start with the basics: what is our agreed response to poor behaviour? What gentle nudges might we use before any reminders or warnings are necessary? When, how and why would we give a reminder or warning to a pupil? What would trigger a child to go on the recognition board? What will we say in public and what is better said in private? What three rules will we both refer to in response to fabulous behaviour and behaviour that needs to be adjusted?

In time, you can unpick the routines together, devise a 30 second script and consider how you are going to use restorative reflection to shift future behaviour. For now, make sure you can meet and greet the class together. Show unity from the door. Play the same first beats. There is nothing worse than having another adult in the room who slips in unnoticed and lurks, unloved, in the back corner. They often spend the lesson asking the children what on earth they are supposed to be learning. They become a wasted resource. When children behave badly, the adults either come to you for the answer or explode at the child before you can say, 'We don't do it like that.' If you don't work on being a team, you will have another human to manage. Someone else taking your time and attention. A potential inconsistency in your perfectly emotionally consistent plan.

Finding the time for discussion after lessons is hard but crucial. Tea, biscuits and a chat go a long way. Picking apart a few positive examples of how it worked well should be accompanied with hard talk about giving Elisha too many chances or giving Carmen too few. It should never be a search for blame but a hunt for the learning that will make it better next time. At first, these are often difficult conversations, so no blame and no judgement are important principles to establish from the start.

THE FIRST BEATS

After the emotionally regulating meet and greet come the first beats of the lesson. As the pupils enter the room, identify – often loudly, sometimes subtly – the behaviour you want to see and acknowledge it. Get busy with it. Bury them in positive affirmations and acknowledgements and the climate of the lesson will begin to take shape. The fastest way to get a class of children to settle is to praise the behaviour you want to encourage. It is easy to bounce from 'I appreciate that, Sam' to 'Great, right place first time, Kiran' to 'Max, you're going straight on the Board of Fame for that – thank you.' Those first interactions are everything. The mood is set and the expectations are reinforced – the teacher 'proper knows what she's doing, fam'. The first beats are amplified and enthusiastic. None of that energy is ever wasted. It is infectious and contagious in the best possible way.

The first beats of positive recognition are a fast and efficient way to communicate your expectations. If they are affirmative and confident, then the emotional climate is established and will wrap around your initial instructions or activity. You can easily find yourself 20 minutes into the lesson without having made a negative observation. It is difficult to start an argument/confrontation/full-scale classroom riot in an atmosphere of appreciative acknowledgement, purposeful activity and high expectations. A positive climate is contagious, but it is not designed to be wheeled in when things start to go wrong. It should be your everyday strategy. After the initial flurry of affirmations the lesson will find a slower pace, but positive nudges are still there in the quietest of reinforcements and non-verbal acknowledgements. The thumbs-up, the sticky note placed on the table as you walk by, the whispered 'Love that' as you return their work. Predictable, consistent and relentless.

DON'T DO THE RULES LESSON

The 'rules lesson' is ubiquitous in many schools, particularly with older students. The idea is to lay out the boundaries from the start (also known as 'laying down the law') so that everyone understands how to behave immediately. Sounds easy, right?

As a head of year, I would beg colleagues not to do the rules lesson on the first day of term. Quite apart from it being the dullest lesson possible and delivered six times for over an hour at a time, it was so at odds with the children's experience when they came for an Open Day or Transition Day. Those lessons were incredible: engaging, memorable, enticing. Exploding science, French food, live performance, even teachers in fancy dress singing about the joys of schooling.

Of course, not every lesson can be a show lesson, but the contrast between seeing the school at its best and seeing the school on rules lesson day was extraordinary. You could see the children's disappointment when you walked into the room: 'Everything alright, Mr Ahmed?' 'Oh yes, Mr Dix, just doing the rules lessons.' The children's eyes were screaming at you: 'Help, please help. We signed up for inspiration – they said it would be fun. We've been mugged off, bruv.' This isn't an argument for making transition days dull and autocratic; it is a plea. I'm begging you – please don't do the rules lesson.

Consistency cannot be established in a single lesson any more than how to behave can be taught in a single lesson. Your students need high expectations, tight routines and essential rules drip-fed over time. Delivering it all at once is as realistic as delivering the entire science curriculum in a double lesson. Break down the rules lesson into smaller pieces and scatter them throughout your teaching in the first two or three weeks. The first day, week or fortnight will likely be a honeymoon of compliance as everyone settles in. A false dawn, certainly, but time enough to space out the learning of behaviour.

Nobody has ever left the rules lesson thinking, 'You know what, that was excellent. I will now be able to behave myself perfectly for the rest of the year.' Especially not those who then walk into exactly the same tragic lesson six times that day and often the next day too. Sheesh.

CO-REGULATING

Relational trauma requires relational repair.

KAREN TREISMAN[2]

The frontal lobe regulates. Damage or late development of the frontal lobe means children can find themselves hijacked by their emotions. It is no longer about 'choice'. Children are not choosing to lose control, they may well not be choosing their behaviour at all. Learning to recognise the difference between children who are making rational choices and those who have temporarily lost their rationale is central. Self-regulating is difficult, complicated and, for some children, an unrealistic expectation. They don't just need you to co-regulate, they cannot do it without you. Putting the punishment away and shifting to support mode is a key skill of an emotionally consistent teacher. You cannot regulate with sanctions, and trying to regulate with rewards has a bad payback.

The greatest example of meeting a child where they are is co-regulating. When supporting behaviour it might be as subtle as gently mirroring physical tension during a conversation or as obvious as lying down next to a child who has taken to the floor in distress. In moments of crisis, threats of punishment are futile. What children need are adults who are not just regulated but who have a flexible, responsive and adaptable plan. Unregulated people don't behave in straight lines.

Many children have difficulty managing their emotions and live surrounded by poor models of self-control. If the solution to being a deregulated adult at home is to take the short cut, grab the drink, punch the wall or kick the dog, then that example slowly percolates into the child. Similarly, if the model is to isolate, withdraw and hide what is happening, the child has no example to learn from or mimic, other than to say nothing.

In areas where poverty has eroded calm families, adults working in schools have the additional pressure of making up for this lost emotional learning. They often need to provide an exaggeratedly perfect model of

---

2   Karen Treisman, *A Therapeutic Treasure Box for Working with Children and Adolescents with Developmental Trauma: Creative Techniques and Activities* (London: Jessica Kingsley, 2017), p. 27.

emotional regulation, and at the same time mop up the fallout from less consistent adult responses. Without regulated adults trying hard to patch the gaps, we risk leaving children emotionally disadvantaged. This is disadvantage that lasts whether or not it is accompanied by academic success, so it is worth the extra time: clambering under a desk to speak to a 5-year-old or yomping across a field to chat to a teenager and climbing the tree where she is chillin'. Adults often need to behave counterintuitively when they recognise a child who is unregulated.

At Firs Primary Academy in Birmingham, head teacher David Shakeshaft knows that the library and, perhaps most importantly, the librarian Rumena Aktar are an essential part of lunchtime regulation for many children – particularly those who are less extroverted. The atmosphere buzzes with the excitement of reading, exploring and gently regulating with books. David speaks highly of his librarian: 'Rumena is an example of over and above – everything she does is driven by a dual love of supporting pupils and the power of reading to unlock the world for them. In these goals, she is relentless.'

The children are safe, relaxed and relieved not to be in the bustle of a busy playground. The library is their safe space: surrounded by books and enriched by the deft interventions and encouragements of an excellent librarian. Libraries were never just for borrowing books, and at Firs it provides a space for much needed pupil support and regulation.

Time pressures in schools, particularly the pressure of giving time to the rest of the class, are very real. It isn't always possible to talk through the door for half an hour to persuade a child to open it or spend most of the morning dealing with a curled-up ball in a coat. Teachers responsible for 30 children need support. Pastoral teams are essential in every school. In areas of social deprivation it should never be low hanging fruit for the cuts of the bean counters. Pastoral support is not a cost, it is an investment. It is work deep in the disadvantage gap. Where support has been stripped out due to cost-cutting, punishment creeps in to try and force the children to regulate – often with disastrous consequences.

Regulated adults develop best in schools where well-being and workload is taken seriously. Toxic school cultures result in stressed adults trying to manage unregulated children. Neither child nor adult wins.

Before trying to help someone else regulate, make sure you regulate yourself:

- Put the punishment clichés away – they won't help.

- Make a plan and be ready to adapt it.

- Be ready not to react to an angry response.

- Frame the situation – that is, calm adult helping distressed child.

- Respect physical space.

- Take away the time limits. 'You have 10 seconds to comply' isn't going to work now.

- Seek the support of key adults who have strong relational currency with the pupil.

- Think about the environment/audience. Is this the best place to help or do you need to move elsewhere?

- Try to offer empathy and not 'solutions'.

- Be ready for many waves of emotion, not a single tidal wave.

- Have a distraction prepared/thought-through.

GROUNDING

For some children, returning to work or routine immediately might be the best way to continue regulating. Often, more time, patience and distraction is helpful, so be ready to walk and talk. As the child begins to regulate, consider using a pre-prepared 'calm box' containing objects and smells that the child knows will help them reconnect with their calm place. There is no magic here but there are comforts and distractions that can help. The box might contain a small soft toy, photo of a family member/friend/pet, fluffy scarf, favourite poem, clicky pen, elastic band for twiddling or squashy ball for squishing. Mike Armiger, legendary educator and amateur Welshman, tells me that for many people peppermint oil (diluted in a carrier like grapeseed or almond oil) in a small rollerball bottle works well for panic and anxiety.

Grounding activities help children to reconnect with the physical world and move away from the looping/enclosing/overwhelming emotions that are driving their behaviour. It can help them to regulate and gives everyone a plan when things get tricky. Callum Wetherill, fellow Lose the Booths enthusiast, works with children with additional needs. He has found that grounding activities are dependent on age. Sensory based activities like drawing, Lego, foam/massage, sand/water and small world play may help younger ones to move through distress. For older children, stuck behind a desk in a crushingly dull careers talk entitled 'Leap into Accountancy', grounding needs to be more subtle: squeezing and releasing the toes, pushing into the chair with back/legs/bottom, holding and pressing on a stone/squashy thing, focusing on relaxing the thumbs completely (I still can't!) or breathing in through the nose for a count of seven and breathing out through the mouth for eleven.

Being sensitive and emotionally responsive to a child's behaviour is so much more than just being calm. The adult also needs to be emotionally available – a skill that requires almost impossible emotional dexterity when trying to teach 29 other children at the same time. Teaching assistants, mentors, pastoral leaders and counsellors can also regulate with the child, so funding matters. If you call for support and the bulb was taken out of the emergency light some time ago, teaching doesn't feel so safe.

Without strong pastoral support, it is unrealistic to expect a teacher to routinely regulate a child struggling with their trauma. The support rarely needs to be permanent; sometimes it could be a while before it is required again. But when a child does need help, patience and an available adult without a deadline, it must be there. Running a false economy and stripping out pastoral support from schools means that teachers and children suffer.

It is difficult to describe the after-effects of trauma, often years later, to someone who has not experienced it. I alighted on the term 'trauma bubbles' to try and communicate how it feels. However, while the randomness of bubble size and unpredictability of bursting seemed to fit, the imagery doesn't quite work. Bubbles are too gentle and too beautiful to describe something that can completely overtake you in the most inconvenient of ways.

The after-effects of trauma can be violent, irrational and certainly unattractive from both the inside and the outside. It is less of a bubble and more a grenade of suffering that arrives without warning, explodes without limits and is totally indiscriminate about who it hurts. The brutality of the imagery might seem over-exaggerated, but from the inside it isn't far off.

Not everyone suffering from trauma responds with anger or violence. It is the loss of control that is so terrifying, whether that displays as tears, withdrawal or the absence of a logical response. It is frightening to those who witness it but also frightening from the inside. With anger, in particular, there is an all-consuming fury that can easily blur the reality of the situation. The feeling of emerging from an episode and not being at all sure how it escalated so far is common. In those moments, there is often nothing that anyone else can do to intervene. Keeping everyone safe until the peak has passed becomes more of a priority.

Recognising that a child is in a state of crisis is vital. Misread this moment and things may quickly spiral out of control.

SOME OF THE CROWD ARE ON THE PITCH ...

Standing on the sideline watching my son play rugby should be the highlight of my weekend, despite the English weather. Regular weekly matches see predictable teams giving each other tight games. On tour, however, things are less predictable.

I am not good at standing on the side of the pitch. I am too competitive, and if I raise my voice in full throated support, it is not long before I find myself slipping into 'over-eager and slightly embarrassing dad' mode.

So far on the tour I had behaved myself. The next under-11 game was against a team from Essex who were a little too 'hands on'. They had the idea that rugby was full contact but hadn't learned to finesse that contact. They were also huge, weighty and up for the rumble. Our team was too polite to be tough – early on in the game we had reported a player for swearing. Things were not going to go well. Two players had already been crushed and taken off and others were playing through tears. It was difficult to watch your team get battered while the referee screamed 'play on'.

As the game progressed and the other team tired, opportunity came knocking. So it was that my son found himself holding the ball in space with the length of the pitch to run and nobody in sight. I rose from my old man's camping chair to cheer and saw that he had a free run to the line. Free apart from that really fast kid with the long legs who was now running at an angle to get to him before the line. Three metres away the fast kid hit him. Not with anything that could even casually be referred to as a tackle. He just ran into him and knocked him out cold, with the ball still in his hand.

I was standing on the sideline, except I wasn't standing on the sideline. I was standing on the pitch, calling the odds, critiquing the referee, having a pop at anyone who challenged me. I think my worst moment might have been shouting at someone who was trying to help and later finding out it was the chairman of our club. In the middle of the shouty chaos I caught a snippet of the other parents muttering in the background: 'Doesn't Paul do behaviour? I'm sure that is how he earns his money! Yes, I think he's a behaviour specialist.' I revived my son and sheepishly walked him off the pitch. We are all capable of reaching 100 mph too quickly. None of us, especially not me, are immune.

Your pupils need your emotional consistency and agility as a constant model of how to be a resilient adult. A teacher's ability to shift their own behaviour to get the best outcomes for their children is as critical as their subject knowledge. Those moments when children need you to step outside the behaviour policy and respond to them on a purely human level matter. Knowing when to hold the boundary with a hard line, when to stretch it and when to let it go come from experience. In behaviour, children are excellent teachers.

STOP THAT!

- Don't fall back on relationships and think that everything will be OK. Fall back on your routines and save your emotional currency for when it is really needed. The conversation you need to have starts with, 'Let's go back to our routine …' and not, 'Come on, Ash – do this just for me.' The latter costs emotional currency; the former is predictable, expected and incurs no debt.

HOW TO LEAD IT

- Watch your own behaviour very carefully. If you are in a leadership role, other adults will take their cue from how you respond to poor behaviour. You cannot afford to slip up in public any more. If you are promoting a shift in adult behaviour, and then are seen to be undermining your own advice, this will allow others to do the same. It is worth being particularly deliberate in your choice of behaviour in assemblies and at other very public times of day. For instance, months of shifting people's attitudes towards positive recognition can be undone in a moment of exasperated shouting at a small child in the front row who then spends the rest of the assembly blubbering until comforted by multiple adults at the end.

- Celebrate consistency in behaviour practice whenever you find it. Your positive and personal recognition of colleagues will drive changes in practice. Notice and appreciate even small changes, such as their willingness to try a 30 second script, persistence at meet and greet or complimenting the positive behaviour of their classes: 'Thank you, Mrs Kinsley, you made that transition so much safer by standing there.' As a leader, the more you catch your colleagues doing the right thing, the faster they will do the same for the children.

NUGGETS

- If you fall off the wagon and have the most inconsistent and emotionally fuelled day, it isn't failure. Sleep, rest, find your calm, consistent and seemingly relaxed alter ego tomorrow morning and go again. Putting starfish back in the sea might seem futile, but every day you still save a starfish.

- Search out the expertise in your school – the teachers and teaching assistants that the children really listen to because they want to, not simply because they are forced to by the hierarchy. Find them, befriend them and learn from them. Search for skills, not seniority or letters after their name. You might be surprised at what the lowest paid member of staff could teach you.

- Simplify everything: focus on just three rules, three ways to positively recognise or three catchphrases/mottos you always use.

He has periodically made an effort.

Paul Dix, school report, age 14

Chapter 2

RECOGNITION REVOLUTION

Recognition is a guaranteed relationship builder. Rewards are hit or miss.

There is a recognition revolution going on in our schools. The big electronic reward systems, along with credit cards packed with 'points for prizes' and gleaming digital arcades of tat, lie like discarded relics of the past, alongside piles of old geography teachers' elbow patches. Things have changed. Reward-heavy teachers are now viewed in the same way as those who cannot see beyond the punishment road. Over-rewarding students has become as distasteful as naming and shaming them.

The dangling carrot has lost its piquancy. Now, nothing whets the appetite like a nice slice of recognition. The enthusiasm for the recognition mechanisms presented in *When the Adults Change, Everything Changes* has filtered through into thousands of classrooms and homes, and the minds of adults. Rewards are unrewarding and recognition is finally getting the recognition it deserves. A new direction has been set.

The biggest shift in classroom and school culture comes with recognition that is focused on effort and applies equally to each child. This might be a mechanism for each class, the whole school, houses or all three. What method you use to record that recognition is less important: it might be a fabulously inviting display on the back of the door, Lego pieces, software with dancing monsters, football cones, fairy wings, fantastic rockets or just a plain old tally strike with a plain old board pen.

If your wall is adorned with the most seductive recognition board complete with lights, klaxon and glitter cannon, that is fantastic, but don't let it become a distraction from the work. Downsizing your recognition board to something more subtle and discreet might be worth considering. The simplest things often work best: taking a lump of play dough from a bucket to add to a zombie face picture or removing a block from a precarious Jenga tower.

I have seen secondary and further education teachers using smiley faces on the smallest of recognition areas on their whiteboard – and the students love it. The less complex your recognition system, the more portable and flexible it is. You might need a mechanism that is easy to move between classes, rooms and situations. A fail-safe sheet of plain A4 paper and a bit of Blu Tack was my go-to portable and adaptable recognition board for years. Teaching four different subjects across many different rooms and three different sites meant that having a fixed all-singing, all-dancing recognition board in one place was impractical.

There have been brilliant adaptations of the recognition board and you can find a growing gallery of them at www.whentheadultschange.com/gallery, including Mickey Mouse, *Toy Story* and even *Frozen* themed recognition boards. Just don't mention it to the Disney lawyers.

Recognition mechanisms are another highly creative, and at times competitive, opportunity for some teachers and just a few names in the corner of the whiteboard for others. I love the creativity and love that goes into making recognition central to the look of the classroom, but I would forgo all of the razzmatazz for a quiet and affirming, 'You have worked so hard today,' and a subtle, unnamed strike on the class tally.

It is easy to tell how far positive recognition is embedded into the fabric of a school, and often how far there is to go. Teachers who wait until the end of the lesson before 'recognising' those who deserve it in public miss so many of the subtle advantages of drip-feeding positive acknowledgement throughout the lesson. Similarly, not using it until an observer enters the room is a common sign that positive recognition is not well developed, perhaps even tokenistic.

If you let positive recognition slide and become random, unplanned or forgotten in the busyness of the classroom, then negative reinforcement will gradually creep back in. The fight against the dark side is real and ever present.

There is no greater driver of a positive and safe classroom than recognition. It changes so much more than the display; it changes adult behaviour. The default becomes to watch for and catch great conduct as opposed to the more typical search for poor behaviour. It matters because everything flows from the classroom. If that can be the safest and the most affirmative place to learn, then it will be the place that children want to be.

In the middle of the busiest classrooms there is time and space for moments of recognition that connect. It is easy to 'perform' a recognition board but it is about so much more than performance. Those moments of appreciation and positive affirmation are the warm Nutella of teaching. The building blocks of relational practice. It is why recognition boards are the most important change you can make in your classroom practice and the most important shift you can make in school policy.

LIQUID BANANA OF SHAME

At a school in Spain, the ubiquitous 'naughty names on the board' was displayed in all its glory. I had grown used to variations on a theme. Teachers are incredibly creative: even when a bad strategy has been imposed on them they work to make it more attractive to the children. Unfortunately, in this room things had gone a little too far.

On the board waiting for the names of children to be written next to them were four bananas in various stages of decay. The first banana, healthy and whole, was proudly positioned at the top of the hierarchy. The second, slightly bruised and withering, sat beneath it; and the third, black and overripe, below that. The last banana in the sequence, at the bottom of the pile, was reserved for the worst behaved children. For their troubles, they had their names written alongside a decayed and melted fruit, which was referred to as 'Liquid Banana'.

My mind wandered to the child returning home from this class to an enthusiastic parent, full of hope that education had inspired their child, to be asked, 'How was your day, son?' 'Liquid Banana, fam, Liquid Banana,' comes the mumbled, shameful reply.

Liquid Banana is not a label that anyone could interpret, let alone respond to, constructively. Nobody benefits from naming and shaming, and casual and ridiculous labelling simply confuses everyone. Liquid Banana is an extreme example, but in many classrooms public humiliation continues unabated, disguised by cartoon imagery to soften the blow. There are still training companies selling the idea of dark clouds and sunshine as if it is evidence based.

The culture of these classrooms is set by naming and shaming on the board: the search is on for the worst behaved child. In these settings, the children who work brilliantly go undiscovered. They are ignored because the focus is on the 5%. Simply avoiding being a Liquid Banana is no recognition at all.

So pervasive is the idea of naughty names on the board that it has even been translated to the animal kingdom. A board in the penguin enclosure at London Zoo identifies the 'naughtiest' penguin of the day. Naughty penguins are named and shamed (Can penguins feel shame? Discuss …) on a daily basis, with different penguins singled out according to an unknown naughtiness scale. Some parents have been heard to note in passing, 'They have the same thing at my daughter's school!'

CREEPING COMPETITION

Recognition systems can easily morph into points or credit based reward systems. Hot Chocolate Friday is a good example. Although the recognition is for children who have been recognised as going over and above, it has been adapted in some settings so that X points equals an invitation or the week's top merit earners get recognised on a Friday breaktime by the head. In individual classrooms, confusion occurs when the appearance of a child's name on the recognition board is linked to positive notes and then positive phone calls home. It quickly becomes a tally of points to earn prizes, and the soul of the idea is lost.

This blending of approaches corrupts the recognition so much that the children who would normally get rewards instead get recognition. Recognition then becomes simply a reward for the best work in comparison to the rest of the class, when it should be the recognition of individual effort and discipline.

Here are five ways to stop recognition from becoming reward:

1. Refocus recognition so that it is solely awarded for effort.

2. Recognition should not be part of a cumulative rewards system.

3. Recognition is collaborative, not competitive.

4. All recognition mechanisms start afresh in a new lesson/session.

5. Shift pupils' thinking towards competing against their best previous efforts, not against each other.

Not everything that can be a competition should be. The competition between schools which is encouraged by political decisions can have perverse outcomes: the branding and copyrighting of the curriculum, restrictions on open sharing between teachers, rivalry to attract the most advantaged children, disincentives to have a fair admissions policy, discouraging vulnerable children/families, dissuading children with special and additional needs, fighting over the 'best' teachers, driving down wages, reducing resources … This list is by no means exhaustive and none of the outcomes seem to benefit the child. When state funded education pretends to be a business there are no clear winners. It seems that the more intense the competition, the worse the outcomes for those most in need.

In individual schools and classrooms, there is a fine line between healthy competition in class for some and systematic daily humiliation for the rest. Many schools try to use competition to motivate, but it rarely works for everyone equally.

If it is a drawing competition, I cannot compete. If it is about punctuality, Ebrahim cannot compete because he has regular hospital visits. If it is an attendance award, Sofia cannot compete because she is a young carer. If it is a drama tournament, Niel's speech and language difficulties will make a podium place more complicated for him. Designing competition in schools and making it fair is not easy. Competitiveness has consequences, usually for those who are already way back on the starting grid, which go unnoticed.

My experience of elite sport is that competition can be exciting, absorbing and healthy. However, at the highest level it is a competition of equals. In schools, where inclusion matters, competition is not equal. A focus on competition inevitably results in an overemphasis on rewards. I have sat in on too many awards ceremonies, year after year, where 1% of the students get 100% of the recognition. Olympic values are great, but introducing intense competition in a school means that the children who are going to lose know they are going to lose before they even hear the starting gun.

ATTENDANCE AWARDS

Attempting to improve attendance using simplistic, competitive award schemes results in a few winners who are already winning and plenty of losers who cannot control their losing. All things being equal, attendance awards are a positive motivator for children to be in school more often. But all things are not equal. Unless safeguards are carefully designed, most attendance awards are ableist and fail any measure of equal opportunity.

How to recognise attendance publicly is fraught with difficulties, particularly for children and families whose ability to attend is compromised: children who have long-term illnesses, additional needs or disabilities. Children who have complicated home lives or addicted parents. Children who are carers or who live in homes where they are the only ones getting up in the morning and have to sift their dirty clothes out of the washing basket. Then there are the children who are urged to stay at home, who have no bus fare or whose lives are so chaotic that you suspect they arrived at school accidentally and not as part of any plan.

Making these children the fall guys for bringing down a class average or allowing their attendance to be highlighted publicly as a failure is not fair or ethical. Neither is it right that a child who attends every possible hour they are able to gets no recognition for their efforts. Raw attendance awards almost certainly do more harm than good. Poor attendance and poverty are old friends. When social support is taken away from families, getting their children to school on time – or at all – becomes less important. Turning it into a competition might seem like a good way to motivate children to feel they are contributing to a team effort. In practice, it pushes the responsibility for attendance on to the child, and that is not a fair place for responsibility to lie.

If you want to improve attendance in your classroom:

- Don't display attendance percentages; instead reinforce classes who achieve their weighted target. 'This class has achieved their target' is all anyone needs to know.

- Make individual attendance targets private, taking into account the child's personal circumstances and needs. The pupil who is only able to attend three sessions a week, and does so, has 100% attendance.

- For younger children who are not in control of their punctuality or attendance, you need to have this conversation with the parent or guardian, not the child. Your positive reinforcement and acknowledgement is best directed at them.

STICKY PRAISE

How you use praise in your classroom makes a difference. Too often, teachers are told to use a ratio of praise or to just wallpaper their classrooms with praise. The initial enthusiasm often wears thin – applauding everything all the time is not only insincere but also utterly exhausting.

Praise works when you acknowledge effort and make it contextual and directed – that is, when it sticks. 'Thomas, you're marvellous' is nice to hear but it isn't sticky. 'Thomas, the effort you've put into your diagram to make it accurate is impressive' is stickier; it is less about the character of the child and more about the success that effort brings. The less motivated or confident the child feels about the task, the more contextual praise is important: 'Thomas, this is an excellent effort from you – almost twice as much done and the quality is consistent. Spot on.'

It is lovely to be in a classroom where praise is everywhere, but it is more productive to be in a classroom where your efforts are sincerely recognised and your character is not in question.

JUDY'S GARLAND

My friend and excellent behaviour expert Darrell Williams told me about a school he visited in Rio de Janeiro, Brazil. He met a group of children in the canteen before the school day and was surprised to see that they were wearing a flower garland. He assumed that it was connected with the Carnival, which was just a few weeks away. However, on further enquiry it became clear that it was more to do with their education than the world's biggest street party.

The children were told that they could keep their garland if they wished, or they could choose to give it to someone else. There were agreed categories for awarding the garland, all of which encouraged the most selfless behaviour. It is fundamentally a well-being strategy, rather than the recognition of more formal behaviours, and it is all the more perfect for it. The categories for recognition (created by the children) were:

- Sticking up for the underdog.
- We know you have been through a tough time.
- We are here for you.
- You have been especially kind.

The process of giving is central to this meta-game. It doesn't happen every day, perhaps once a fortnight or once a month.

The children, without a thought of keeping their own garland, sought to bestow it on one of their classmates. They were fair and responsible with their choices and didn't just award them to their friends. The giving of garlands ebbed and flowed at different times during the day. Children finding themselves with multiple garlands would try to distribute them and those without a garland looked for opportunities to help or be kind. Of course, receiving a garland necessitated a bow and a moment of authentic connection between the children.

This certainly wasn't the first time the children had been given the garlands, but it didn't distract from their learning. Rather, they were gently co-regulating and creating their own positive reinforcement and affirmation. It was a visible, peer-led recognition mechanism that held the children's interest all day. They were quite clear that the adults should not intervene with the garland-giving.

Was this Brazilian behavioural nirvana or a simple recognition system that could be replicated in your own setting? Darrell told groups of teachers about the garlands and they started experimenting by using wristbands instead of garlands – with similar results.

The next level for the recognition board might not be more flashing lights, confetti cannons or positive klaxons, but tweaking the system so the children have a shared responsibility – or even ownership – of it. This leaves the teacher, who previously needed to put a great deal of energy into 'working' the recognition board, free to pass over a great deal of work to the children. It strikes me that shifting the categories for recognition towards well-being encourages exactly the kind, considerate behaviour that everyone wants to see.

It seems that 'first attention for best conduct' is not just a behaviour strategy. The moment of giving and gratitude stimulates the serotonin buzz, positive dopamine loop and emotional connection that makes everyone feel like Carnival. (Oh, and one of the children was definitely called Judy or the heading wouldn't work, would it!)

RECORDING RECOGNITION

In some settings, there is an obsession with recording every behaviour, even the really small ones. The idea is that behavioural changes can be identified earlier and intervention can be more targeted. In reality, it means a huge amount of work for the teacher. This inevitably results in negative points also being diligently documented. There isn't a positive balance. A database of bad news doesn't help anyone to help the child. The small stuff in lessons doesn't need to be detailed, entered into a computer and forever filed against the pupil's name. Record only the point at which the child is removed from the room; everything else is of no real interest to anyone except you and the pupil.

If you spend your time recording every behaviour, you can find yourself devoting more time to data entry than building positive relationships. If you do want to document classroom recognition, emulate Mrs McLean's example at St Patrick's Primary School in Greenock, Scotland, and get yourself a 'recognition frame'. Photograph your pupils with their heads poking through the frame and the behaviours they are being recognised for written underneath. Alternatively, Miss Armstrong, deputy head teacher at Boghall Primary School in West Lothian, has a display board in her office titled 'Miss Armstrong's Proud Patches' featuring photographs of every pupil with their fabulous work in clear plastic pockets.

CORRIDOR RECOGNITION

Most recognition is not recorded but it is no less important. Moments of transition in a school, when footfall is greatest, represent an opportunity to check in with children, to be visibly and audibly consistent, and to relentlessly reinforce the positive climate.

School corridors that ring with positive recognition set a safe and purposeful climate that leaks into every classroom. Senior leaders, non-teaching staff and pastoral leaders can make a huge difference in the corridors even if they aren't meeting and greeting at a classroom door. Standing on the same spot at the same time every day is positive, visible consistency.

The subtle reinforcement of great behaviour is a good start and notches up the good stuff. Louder, less personal pronouncements mean everything: 'I love the patience being shown here – thank you for keeping the stairs safe.' 'Perfect and on time, all of you – fantastic.' The kindness of the recognition gives everyone a warm glow. Passing this over to the teachers waiting at their classroom doors is then easy: 'Mr Dunn, these are the finest students I have met today. They look utterly ready to learn.' Calm corridors support every teacher and make for the calmest meet and greet.

Dishing out generous helpings of positive reinforcement in public means that it becomes an accepted part of the school culture. It eases the way in to conversations with individuals and makes recognition boards a more natural step. It also gives permission to every adult to do the same. Done well, it is a fabulous model of adult behaviour and it is infectious.

PLAYGROUND RECOGNITION

The best midday supervisor transformation I have seen was at Newtongrange School in Dalkeith. Head teacher Vicky Morgan and the team had already enthusiastically launched a behaviour revolution. The meet and greet and recognition board culture in classrooms had been a huge success but they were struggling to bring in the midday staff. They were outliers and needed to be included in the changes before the gap became a chasm. As in many schools, the part-time staff didn't have the same access to training or new ideas. It is difficult to ask for more hours from part-time staff and hard to coordinate for everyone to be in a training session at the same time. It requires innovation.

Newtongrange saw training everyone as a priority. They made time and energy to coach their midday staff so that they understood the 'why' and not just the 'how'. The midday supervisors liked the idea of a recognition board and could appreciate how it worked well in classrooms, but they couldn't see how it might help them to manage playtime behaviour. A large board in the playground might be alright for a couple of weeks of the Scottish summer (basically the whole summer) but it was not practical all-year round.

However, the school found a brilliant workaround. A large prominent board near reception was given over to playtime recognition. The children, like recognition meerkats, were immediately on their toes straining to see. The sign on the board read:

Throughout our breaktimes you can earn links for our Whole School Recognition Board when you demonstrate our positive playground expectations. When our chain reaches 1,000 links we will have a special whole school treat.

(This was vague enough to keep all options open.) The playground expectations were also posted up:

- Be considerate and cooperative with others.
- Use kind words.
- Use equipment safely and properly and return it in good condition.
- Share space with others.
- Follow the rules of the game and be a good sport.
- Stay in the school grounds.
- Respond to bell times.
- Put rubbish in the bins.

Each midday supervisor was given 10 paper chain links to hand out at lunchtime. The children who had earned them proudly linked them to the lengthening chain on the display. Each day the children strove to be recognised for the right behaviours and each day the chain grew.

A simple strategy that has a huge impact. The focus for the midday supervisors changed overnight. Instead of spending lunchtime trying to weed out the children who were not behaving well, they were now looking for the children going over and above – those who were defusing arguments, playing generously and helping others. From the moment the first link was given out, the children engaged with the strategy. By the end of the first week, the links and chain were creating a great deal of interest and excitement. The children wanted the board to be completely covered in paper chains. Reinforcing the new scheme and sharing success in assembly also gave the strategy the status it needed.

The midday staff loved the change in direction. They started enjoying their jobs again and their role as playground enforcers was gone forever. Relationships have flourished, playground behaviour has been transformed and arguments that used to spill over into classrooms and spoil the learning have disappeared. The children responded brilliantly and were proud of the links they earned, but also the links earned by others. The midday supervisors are now a joined-up part of the team effort. Every adult leads behaviour.

HOT CHOCOLATE FRIDAY EXPLODES!

The sustained success of Hot Chocolate Friday (#HotChocFri) leads me to two conclusions. Firstly, Hot Chocolate and Fridays were meant to be together. Secondly, everyone, especially adults, loves positive recognition. The 15 minutes on a Friday morning breaktime have been incorporated into the rhythm of school life, and head teachers continue to tell me that it is their favourite 15 minutes of the week.

Variants continue: from Tea Tuesday and Popsicle Friday to digital Hot Chocolate Online and Prosecco Friday (for staff – but not at morning break!). Healthy alternatives are also available: Fruity Friday and Friday Crackers have been popular, although Gruel Tuesday has not taken off so well in more grumpy schools.

When I visit schools I am often introduced as 'the man who invented Hot Chocolate Friday'. Every time, the children stop listening at 'chocolate' and I have to explain that I didn't invent chocolate before a chocolate riot starts. 'Er, Daz … see that bloke over there – turns out he flippin' invented chocolate!' 'Tidy, let's go rob him.'

For one head teacher, Russell Ingleby, who leads Hightown Junior, Infant and Nursery School in West Yorkshire, Hot Chocolate Friday was missing a few people who really mattered. In a determined attempt to involve even the most reluctant parents in celebrating their child's efforts, he decided to visit the home of one child a week to celebrate Hot Chocolate Friday at home. The news of the special visit was halfway around the estate before he had opened the biscuits, and the chance of a visit quickly became top currency. Hot Chocolate Friday at home works so well because it squares the circle. A parent hearing about something special happening at school bears no comparison to the head teacher turning up on the doorstep with a packet of Jammie Dodgers, a sachet and a smile.

At Kent College Dubai, deputy head Andy Parkin has sustained Hot Chocolate Thursday (Fridays are a holiday in the UAE) throughout the COVID-19 pandemic. Alongside some real shifts in adult behaviour has come a policy revolution. That the school rules are 'wonderful walking', 'tremendous transitions' and 'marvellous manners' shows deep commitment to the highest standards, and not just a shared obsession with alliterative adjuncts. The school sees Hot Chocolate Thursday as a key part of the changes:

We are quite a big school (around 37 classes from Foundation Stage 1 to Year 6) so we aren't able to provide hot chocolate to every child in every class. However, nominations for the week, and why, are a required point on all year groups' weekly agendas. Pre-COVID, the nominated children would come and have lunch with me in our school canteen where I would make and serve them all a mug of hot chocolate with marshmallows (optional). The children loved it! It was lovely to see the older children asking the younger ones why they had received it.

This understanding of 'why' is important to me as children need to be able to articulate what it is they should be proud of, especially when they go home and parents ask them. Due to COVID I can't get all the children together any more but we still keep it going. I now hand-deliver certificates along with personal sachets of hot chocolate so the children can make it at home with their parents. The impact of introducing this has been incredible. All the children want it – and because the teachers make a point of explaining why, I feel other children step up and want to earn it too.

ANDY PARKIN, DEPUTY HEAD TEACHER, KENT COLLEGE DUBAI

POSITIVE NOTES 2.0

The regular, consistent and proportionate use of positive notes remains the simplest and most impactful strategy to connect and reinforce success at school with home. The beta version of the positive note home is perfect in its simplicity: plain white card with a handwritten message.

However, left in the hands of creative teachers it was always going to be radically embellished. Positive notes have become 'legend cards' and 'superhero news'. 'Have a brew on me' cards are given out in one school when students are caught doing the right thing. They are exchanged in the cafeteria for a cup of tea. In other settings, 'Ask me why I got this' stickers mean the child has a memorable day of acknowledgement, while positive notes with scannable QR codes allow parents and carers to see the work that has been recognised.

There are 'You are amazing' cards and beautiful 'Good news' cards on pure white embossed cardboard that look like an invitation to a royal wedding. Of course, there are digital replacements too, but the tactile nature of a physical note, coupled with the care of a handwritten message, can mean everything to a parent. However, there is a subtle balance to be struck between the appropriate use of positive notes and overuse that wrecks the currency. If you see positive notes crumpled at the bottom of school bags or left on the desk, then you might be overdoing it. Just one positive note every week from each adult works very well.

Designing and embedding a recognition culture into the heart of a school takes time and energy. There are always tweaks and adjustments that keep it interesting for the children. At Arthur Bugler Primary School in Essex, head teacher John Bryant invites children who receive positive notes to spin a wooden wheel of destiny to see if they can win some extra playtime for their class. The Ikea inspired spinning wheel is the icing on the cake of a suite of positive interventions at Arthur Bugler. The positive phone calls home are regular and cherished; the school climate reverberates with positive recognition, acknowledgement and praise; Friday assemblies are exuberant; and the word 'fun' is spread about liberally. The school climate drives achievement, attendance and relational practice. It is joyful – like all good education should be.

NEW DAY, NEW CLIMATE

Assuming that because you had a good lesson yesterday that today's will be great too has tripped up all of us. You walk away from the crime scene of the lesson desperately trying to work out why the behaviour you thought had been buried rose up from the zombie grave and bit your arm off.

Just as each day is a clean sheet, so each day is an opportunity to rebuild and reinforce. In fact, if you don't start from scratch in every lesson, particularly in the first term, you risk some pupils forgetting your high expectations or bringing unwanted behaviours with them.

Rebuild the positive climate every lesson, make a point of it and soon the children will bring it with them. That means:

▪ Meeting and greeting.

▪ Recognising the behaviour you want immediately.

▪ Reminding them of the boundaries before setting off on each task.

▪ Deliberately and persistently searching for positive behaviour.

▪ Making sure the last thing they hear is a positive affirmation of the good things.

Positive recognition changes the daily climate. It fuels relationships, trust and individual self-esteem. It forces shifts in language and expectation while making everyone feel good. Nobody enjoys working in an environment that seeks only to squash bad behaviour, where the threat of punishment forces a wedge between children and adults. The most significant change you can make in behaviour practice is positive acknowledgement. Expend your energy on positive strategies, refreshing and renewing them to keep the interest high. The solution to your behaviour problem is never going to be found in consequences; it lies in your ability to pick up on the good stuff unrelentingly.

STOP THAT!

▪ Giving some children recognition so they don't feel left out. Focus on effort, not achievement, and make sure they know the behaviour you are looking for. There is no 'my turn to win'.

▪ Offering recognition in exchange for a specific action. It is just bribery.

HOW TO LEAD IT

- Having a recognition mechanism in each classroom that is visible doesn't mean that it actually gets used.

- Support its use in class when you visit by finding a child to recognise who is going over and above. Encourage colleagues to give pupils control over the recognition board so it takes minimal effort from the adults.

- The more positively you behave towards good behaviour, the more others are given permission to do the same. Just as a teacher creates the climate in their lesson, so leaders create the climate in their school.

NUGGETS

- Recognise colleagues discreetly, generously and often. A secret Hot Chocolate Staff Friday never goes unappreciated. Handwritten notes celebrating effort never get thrown away. Genuine recognition and acknowledgement should not be used to make an example of one staff member over another. Private is almost always better.

- Visitors to your setting should hear the positive recognition before they see it. If adults are reinforcing great behaviour, the corridors will be thick with acknowledgement, appreciation and kindness. When the 95% know they will get noticed first and noticed consistently, it is their behaviour that becomes normalised.

- One positive note, one positive call home, every week, every adult.

- Quiet recognition is a beautiful thing; not everyone wants their efforts advertised.

Contributes almost nothing to the lesson. He obviously understands little and learns even less.

Paul Dix, school report, age 13

Chapter 3

PROPORTIONATE AND PRODUCTIVE CONSEQUENCES

If blind obedience in the classroom is king, then there is scant chance of a positive relationship.

After some years of working with schools to establish successful relational practice, I had created a compelling evidence base. Next, I wanted to accelerate the pace of change and show people with influence the transformations that had taken place in some previously chaotic schools. Perhaps they could share the practice – maybe even learn something from it. I wrote a letter to the then shadow schools minister, Nick Gibb. The political winds were about to blow in a Conservative government (a coalition, as it turned out) and I anticipated that he was about to take on responsibility for behaviour in schools. I didn't expect a response and was a little shocked that he was prepared to meet with me. To be honest, the thought of going alone was a little terrifying. I had never had a meeting with an MP, so I contacted my friend Bill Gribble, of whom I have always been in awe of his experience in the field of behaviour. Bill, a proud socialist, was more than wary about meeting a Conservative shadow minister, but I tried to persuade him that it was for the greater good.

So it was that Bill and I found ourselves waiting outside a room in the Palace of Westminster. I was nervous, Bill not at all. I tried to give a small pep talk before we went in: 'Now, Bill – these people are full-on Conservatives, no holds barred. If you could possibly rein in your politics a little and focus on the behaviour issue …' He seemed to have heard me, but Bill is his own man.

The conversation started badly. I am not sure it could have been any worse. Nick Gibb immediately launched into a rant about the social and emotional aspects of learning. He claimed they were utter nonsense and he was determined to remove them entirely from the system. Knowing that Bill's life's work had been spent promoting exactly what the shadow minister seemed to despise, I was kicking Bill under the table to try and stop him from biting, but it was too late. He immediately unmasked himself and there was a sharp exchange of views. Nick Gibb then deliberately turned away from Bill and focused on me.

I explained that there was strong evidence from across a huge range of schools that my approach reduced exclusions, increased learning time and led to a significant drop in lesson removal. I talked my heart out about relational practice, trust and mutual respect in schools. I was halfway through describing how it had positively impacted on staff workload, children's behaviour and parental engagement when he'd had enough. He banged the table with a fist, jabbed his finger at me and shouted, 'I've just been to six military schools, Paul. I WILL TELL YOU ABOUT BEHAVIOUR.' For a chartered accountant he seemed awfully angry.

And so here we are 12 years later. In English schools, there are record high exclusions, a crisis in children's mental health, isolation booths, a variety of cruel and unusual punishments being permitted by the back door, and schools picking the children they want and those they don't. The moral of the tale? Allowing education policy to be driven by a right-wing chartered accountant isn't going to turn out well.

As we walked back to the Tube station Bill said it had been a fabulous day out and he had thoroughly enjoyed the meeting. 'But, Bill, we got nowhere,' I protested. 'Yes,' said Bill, 'but I knew that before we arrived.' Lesson learned.

BEING FAIR AND RESPECTING RIGHTS

It is easy to arrive at a point where the proportionate response is no longer the norm. After all, if the punishment isn't working, the temptation is to punish more, punish harder. I explored the madness of picking up bigger sticks in *When the Adults Change, Everything Changes* (chapter 7). Grasping for increasing levels of punishment means that responses to poor behaviour can become disproportionate. At this point things change. As trust in the school's fairness weakens, the support of parents wobbles, children stop focusing on their behaviour and instead on the scale of punishment, and everyone entrenches in their position. The school often protests that they can't possibly shift their standards for one student, the parents argue against high levels of punishment for minor misdemeanours and the child is confused.

I don't think the confusion comes from the sight of the adults disagreeing – they do that all the time – but from the contradiction at the heart of the response. Fairness and rights are important concepts taught by teachers and parents. We soak children in compelling stories that demonstrate the injustice of disproportionate responses (Rosa Parks, Nelson Mandela, Martin Luther King, Ai Weiwei, Harvey Milk, Jesus, for Christ's sake) and then expect them not to question their own experience of punishment. A proportionate response is the right response, be it global news or the talk of Year 5. In schools where proportionality has been lost, there is a relational chasm between the stakeholders.

The recent volte-face by significant groups of charter schools in the United States on restrictive classroom routines, punitive behaviour systems and high exclusions is a positive development. They are to be applauded for the changes, even though there is a huge slice of 'told you so' coming from every educator who saw the flaws years before. Consistency needs to be achieved ethically or it is meaningless. Directing children's gaze, the way they hold their hands on the desk or how they speak are signs of control, not discipline.

Some schools keep their classroom consistency cruelly simple. Their 'non-negotiable' classroom behaviour protocol contains just two steps: C1 (warning) and C2 (24 hours of isolation). As a response to low level behaviour it is screamingly disproportionate.

It sounds like the perfect utopia for a teacher (just don't mention the excluded): skipping in and delivering reams of glorious knowledge without a whimper of challenge (no, really don't mention them) and gathering plaudits from far and wide (seriously, shut up about those children). Of course, there are no miracles. Each and every time, the children who fall through the net are casually forgotten. When did adults have to suffer such disproportionality? I am not sure there is any teaching union in the world that would endorse 'one warning, then suspension' for its members. Unsurprisingly, an unethical behaviour policy produces rampantly unethical outcomes. Success created on the backs of the isolated and excluded is not success. It is a problem passed on to someone else. Adults do some strange things and call it behaviour management.

There is an ethical approach to dealing with behaviour that punishment rich and empathy poor behaviour systems wilfully ignore. Shifting adult behaviour cannot be simply an appeal for better emotional self-regulation. There needs to be system change. A hard look at how and why children are removed from classrooms is essential in any school. Couple this with a process for those who need to leave the room, which is designed to be productive, corrective and return students to learning, and the climate shifts.

In a desperate bid for consistency, sanctions are applied to even the youngest children. I regularly see tariff sheets listing the most minor behaviours. It is supposed to be a coverall for every adult to refer to, except nobody does. It's always an approximation. 'Right, one demerit for "walking around the room", plus two demerits for "boffing Rizwan on the head", plus, er, about four for … that will be, let me see …'

Tariff lists limit the teacher's ability to deal with behaviour as they see it. Micromanaged consistency breeds inconsistency because teachers resent the control and limitation.

THE *NEW* CLASSROOM SUPPORT PLAN

When I was asked to work with two schools in the North West of England from Holy Family Catholic Multi Academy Trust, the challenge was simple to express: to reduce exclusion, increase effective inclusion and raise standards of behaviour in the classroom. Both schools had a zero tolerance, tariff/removal room and punishment rich history; one school had imposed it on the other. There were signs of blood on the carpet, but new chief executive officer Andy Moor had done a great job of trying to scrub it clean. Fixed-term exclusions were running at an alarming rate, but everyone was still frustrated with the standards of behaviour and the limitations that policy had on understanding pupil needs.

At the heart of the matter was the rate of removal from classes and the increasing amount of time children spent in removal rooms, which in turn was overloading the system and pushing up fixed-term exclusions. The answer was not to cap exclusions and retrofit a behaviour policy, but to reduce removal and release the bottleneck of children moving up the exclusion escalator.

Refining classroom behaviour plans to support pupils who are struggling to stay within the rules needs lots of time to develop and lots of consulta-tion to ensure everyone understands their role. However, a whole school shift from isolation and removal rooms to a more bespoke response often doesn't require more funding or more staffing. It just needs an adjust-ment in the plan and a change in behaviour from all the adults involved in the process.

Intervening and redirecting behaviour is rarely as simple as moving through a hierarchy of steps until the child decides to back away. Your behaviour is influential here. There are 1,000 ways to deliver a warning, for instance, ranging from a gentle and affirming 'Just watch yourself' to full-on clipboard and big tick 'Riiiiiight, I believe *that* is a warning.' Of course, the mechanism is less important than the delivery, but it is worth getting it right. The alternative is having no structure around con-sequences, which often results in too many warnings ('Altaf, this is your seventeenth warning – I won't warn you again'), too many randomly invented punishments ('Well, you'll have to stay in at lunchtime until you can say sorry') and too many arguments about fairness ('You let

Noori out to play straight away [covered in paint] and I [also covered in paint] am cleaning the classroom with the toothbrush again. I'm calling my lawyer!').

Steps enable you to keep your response to behaviour proportionate, they are predictable for the pupils and make it easier for you to keep track of the behaviour of 35 children simultaneously. A stepped approach is not perfect, but don't let perfect be the enemy of good.

You might choose to display the classroom support plan, but it shouldn't simply be a replacement for 'punishment steps'. It is more nuanced: less about trying to allocate punishment and much more about giving support. It is not there to point at and announce, 'If you don't behave you will be sent to triage.' If you are going to put the plan on the wall, the children will need to know how it differs from punishment steps and you will need to treat it differently too.

Let's take each aspect of the support plan in turn and explore how to use it. The first steps are ones that you might use already, but even these moments can be refined.

REMINDER

A good reminder is not a casual aside; it is more pointed. Redirect the pupil to the agreed boundaries for the lesson/task. Ask the child to recall them if time allows.

WARNING AND A MINUTE

You can place a bit more emphasis on the warning, perhaps punctuated with a positive and/or giving the child up to a minute of positive attention to help them back on track.

TWO MINUTES AFTER THE LESSON

Speaking to the teacher for up to two minutes at the end of the lesson is the main thing the child will remember. There is a temptation to read the riot act and give them the old 'If you do that just one more time' speech,

CLASSROOM SUPPORT PLAN (SUMMARY)

Calm and easy on every step, with plenty of take-up time. Resist the urge to jump steps.

Reminder

Take-up time …

Warning and a minute

Take-up time …

Last chance, script and two minutes after the lesson

Lots of take-up time …

Triage or departmental support

Teacher's choice

Quick catch-up, restorative conversation, imposition, detention or natural consequence

Serious breaches

These are behaviours that will result in immediate triage[1]

---

1 See page 58 for more on serious breaches.

but it is worth considering how you want the child to leave. It may well affect how they arrive at the beginning of the next lesson.

Angry children arriving at dingy punishment rooms with grumpy adults is not the most innovative approach for helping children to regulate. It is all too common for behaviour to deteriorate further on entering such rooms, particularly if they perceive the culture within it to be more unreasonable than the one they have just left. This can be further exacerbated by additional restrictions and rules. The expectation seems to be that if you cannot manage your behaviour in the classroom, then we will manage it for you when you arrive in the removal room. There is an irritation built into the system, as well as an unrealistic expectation that children who have been dysregulated in one context will immediately be able to regulate, on their own, when they arrive in another. This is where the Orwellian 'If you fail the consequence room then …' comes in.

TRIAGE

Triage is a no-blame environment. Shifting to the triage model might be the most positive change to managing classroom removal you can make.

Triage must address the question: 'How can we return this student to their next class, calm and ready to learn?' But it cannot also answer the questions that arise from their exit from the previous lesson, and nor should it. The class teacher may need and want to speak to the student because it is their lesson they will be walking into tomorrow. Picking up your own tab is the responsibility of the class teacher. Relational practice stumbles without this connection.

As we can see from the diagram on page 53, there are four key principles to the triage approach:

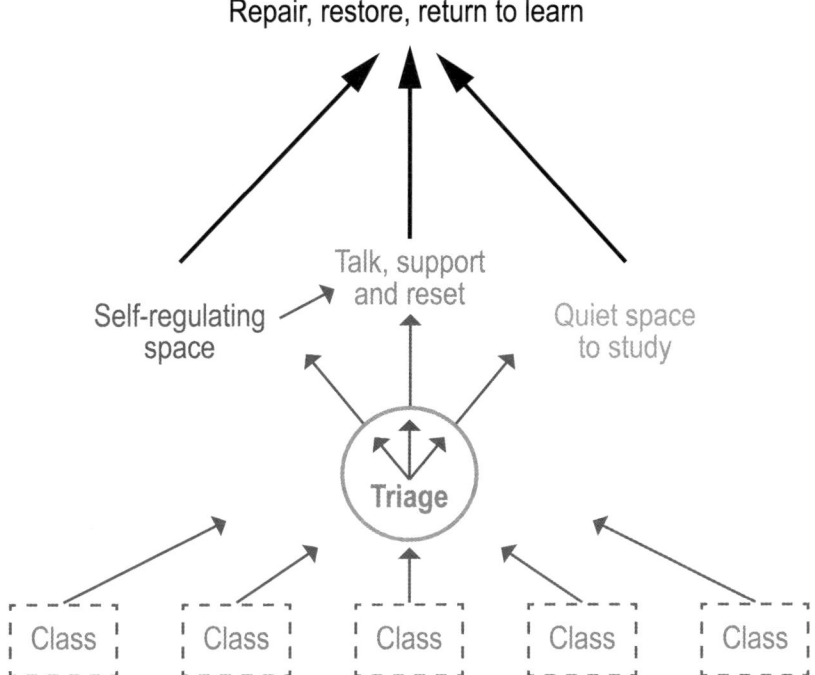

Key principles

▪ Triage is a no-blame environment

▪ Students stay for one lesson only

▪ Class teachers follow up when necessary

▪ Being removed from class is a consequence

1. Triage is a no-blame environment

When students arrive at triage there should be no blame and no judgement, regardless of the nature of the incident. This is critical. When you arrive at the police station after arrest, the line is clearly drawn by the custody sergeant: 'We are not here to judge you. We have had no involvement in your arrest. This is about process.'

I am not suggesting that triage should mimic a custody suite in design or restriction of liberty, but it is an interesting separation of duties. It means that the anger attached to the arrest is dissipated and allows everyone to start afresh. 'What do you need?' rather than 'What on earth have you done?' This principle is really useful in a school. It helps everyone to compartmentalise the incident and move on to the next stage. It also means that children expect to be met by adults who seek to help rather than those who might be cross with them. That changes how they behave when they arrive at Triage and *nobody needs to be angry*.

2. Students stay for one lesson only

There may be exceptions when we need to keep a student for a bit longer – we can all think of at least a couple – but that doesn't mean we should not establish high expectations. If the system is set up to hold children for days and weeks, then it can also be set up to reduce the time they are out of lessons. Keeping children out of class all day for a minor incident in lesson one makes no sense. It is not a system designed to return children to learning; it is purely punishment based. In most settings, it will contradict the important messaging on attendance and that every lesson counts.

Devise the removal/reintegration process to be efficient, impactful and kind from the ground up. If you only had 20 minutes to return a student to learning, how would you design the process?

3. Class teachers follow up when necessary

Follow-up is time-consuming and irritating. It often feels that life is too busy and that someone else should deal with poor behaviour. The truth is that following up is central to your consistency. It gives you the opportunity to reset expectations for the next lesson, address the difficulties from the last one and, perversely, it helps to build relational currency. After all, not everyone bothers to follow up because not everyone wants to look the student in the eye. Some teachers choose not to do so and then complain vigorously when nothing has changed.

4. Being removed from class is a consequence

Asking a child to leave the class is not a moment to be taken lightly.

Now we are at the heart of it. I can feel some of you screaming at the page and others whooping in agreement. This statement needs some context. Removal may not be the only consequence, of course. Smashing up a computer, denting Michael's face or telling the teacher they are a 'cockwomble' will certainly require further action. Yet most children who are asked to leave a class have done nothing so extreme. Many have been repeatedly off task, ignored instructions or had a disagreement with a classmate. It is a well-worn path. Perhaps we could just change the language from 'being sent out' or 'removed' or, even worse, 'excluded from class' and call it what it really is – a chance for a student to get some more support.

It is hard to make a logical argument that a child who needs support in one lesson for apparent crimes should be banned from lessons for the rest of the day. Proportionate responses are essential. Adults who want more punishment for minor crimes must be satisfied with the logical and proportionate response. Anything else is just emotion.

Triage is not a step towards punishment or an escalator to another hierarchy of pain. It is a chance to meet the needs of the student. In maths it would be called 'same day intervention'. The support available should work with the child. This is not necessarily a moment to try and control them more, to ratchet up the threat or to impose a raft of tighter restrictions.

A genuine attempt to work *with* needs a different lens. Communicating your expectations for students arriving at triage is vital. They need to know how they will be helped. In this context, a better starting point is 'What does this child need?' It is a better starting point for triage than 'What has this child done?'

Print out the text below and give it to children arriving at triage so they know exactly what to expect.

Information for students

You have arrived at triage.

Expect to be here for up to 30 minutes or until the end of the next lesson.

Our job is to help you get back to learning. None of the adults at triage have anything to do with what has just happened. They are not responsible for consequences. They won't talk to you about why you are out of class unless you want to.

What happens next?

There are four choices available at triage. You may be asked to choose or you may be directed to one or the other by the adults:

1. Self-regulating space.
2. Talk, support and reset.
3. Quiet space to study.
4. Revolving door.

We are here to get you ready for the next lesson.

In primary schools and smaller schools, triage can take place in the corridor rather than in a separate room. A desk to work at quietly, time to self-regulate using a cushion or walking along a snake designed into the carpet, a den to hide in for a minute or two. There are good examples of self-regulating spaces in the corridors of Danish schools. They are designed into the learning environment and everyone accepts that any child might need them and choose to use them. Children might be sent there, but more often they take themselves there and learn, with support, to manage their own emotions. When there are just one or two children wobbling in your class, the strategy can be more personal and designed to return the child to the class rather than remove them from all lessons.

When children arrive at triage, some will benefit from silence and separation, some will need talking down, some will need explanation, meditation or inspiration. Much of this can be difficult to read in the classroom, particularly if you and the class are new to each other. Triage that seeks to deliver a tailored response does not undermine the teacher; it is the logical path.

Self-regulating space

The self-regulating space isn't a windowless storeroom where a voice periodically shouts through a hatch, 'Are you calm yet?' It doesn't display neon posters that demand: 'Think about what you have done!' or 'Dream about being better!' It should be a calm space where children can breathe and compose their emotions. In practice, this room is requested more often than you might imagine. Children, like adults, need a bit of private time and space to compose themselves, or at least to begin that process.

Talk, support and reset

Talk, support and reset is a one-to-one coaching conversation that supports the child to continue regulating and prepares them for the next part of their day. It might take just a few minutes before they are ready to move to a quiet space to study or it might take longer.

Occasionally, triage will lead to a revolving door and the student will be sent to their next lesson within a few minutes. These exceptional cases might be a student removed at the end of a lesson whose best chance of recovery lies not in another 30 minutes in the quiet study space, but being there at the beginning of the next lesson with a strong adult influence.

Quiet space to study/work room

This room is not part of the punishment but a place to work for a few minutes and show readiness to return to lessons. This cannot be a place to hold children who need to be out of lessons for longer. On these rare occasions, the child should be supervised away from triage with a key adult or head of department.

TEACHER'S CHOICE

Give teachers control over consequences. They know their students best, so they should have authority and not have it usurped by someone else applying blanket policies. When the teacher has the power to decide, the child stops looking over their shoulder for a higher authority. Obviously, if they are the sort of teacher who, given the choice, always reaches for the same consequence then they will need support in differentiating their response.

Sometimes it is not about choosing one option from the list but a combination. The child who is rude to their teacher might need to stay in at break, but (as trust is clearly weak) don't miss the opportunity for a restorative chat. Similarly, a quick catch-up might be a prelude to the child clearing up the mess they have made. A good behaviour policy encourages problem-solvers not process monkeys. You want colleagues to see a behaviour, see the child, gauge the context and act. Responding with, 'Hold on, let me check page 18 of the punishment tariff to see what I should do …' just weakens a teacher's authority. Children quickly recognise those adults who just want to 'apply the policy' and those who are more considered in their response.

A *quick catch-up* might take place in the yard, in the canteen or an opportune meeting in the corridor. It is just a check-in to see that the student is OK, that there is nothing more to clear up and, perhaps, an opportunity for them to apologise. It is an informal conversation.

Restorative conversations should be used in the right circumstances, usually when trust or respect have been strained.

Impositions are work that is taken home to complete and signed by the parent/guardian. If the student spent the lesson pretending to work (and they understood what they were supposed to be doing) then give them the work to do at home. Children who regularly turn up for detentions will regularly complete impositions. The only difference is that you haven't wasted your time supervising them.

Detention is such an ugly word. Adults often think that children fear detentions. The truth is that at 14 you aren't terribly busy and are default immortal. Taking an hour from a 14-year-old when they have the whole expanse of time and space to play in isn't a deterrent. Keep a child in for five minutes at breaktime or during lunchtime, but let's not pretend it is the right solution for most children. The majority of children need a chat, a reset or a reflection with an adult, not to sit in silence supervised by an adult.

Natural consequences are simple: clean up the mess you made, put right what you did wrong, fix the thing you broke. If there is a natural consequence, use it. Throwing a can of pop around in the corridor and then sitting in detention feels like you got away with it. Getting on your hands and knees and scrubbing the floor clean feels proportionate and just.

SERIOUS BREACHES

There will be some behaviours that are a threat to the emotional or physical safety of others and beyond any steps. Some of these behaviours will depend on your context, while others – racism, violence, homophobia – are universals. If a serious breach occurs, there are no warnings or reminders. The pupil is moved to triage immediately. To protect the victims of a particularly nasty incident, a serious breach might see the child separated for longer. Sometimes children cannot return to learning within the target time; in fact, it would be harmful to do so.

When you shift to a triage model without having significantly improved communication between the triage team, class teachers and head of department/faculty, it puts stress on teachers, as they will want to follow up and decide on next steps with the pupil. If there is not a seamless feedback loop, particularly in a large secondary school, then a pupil can reappear at the next lesson without any resolution to the behaviour in the previous lesson. Nobody wants this as it sends all the wrong messages. If your school lacks an elegant digital solution, then a five-minute check-in with the head of department at the end of the day is the best approach. In this way, the triage team have one line of communication to the department and pupils don't get missed. In-day resolutions are always preferable, even if it means making that call home which starts, 'I don't want to keep you long but …'

Behaviour and relationships are, for some, annoyingly nuanced. The arguments around consequences for poor behaviour are always focused on the extremes. It seems to be either all the punishment or none of it. The truth is that there are subtle differences that can nudge productive consequences into punitive sanctions. Left unchecked, this can normalise the punitive and unbalance the system. It is the difference between 30 minutes out of class to deal with the problem and a whole day stewing in isolation, or between a quick call to mum to sort out the earrings and 'You are out of lessons for the rest of the week/month/year until you take them off'. The reason this is so important is that it is easy for a system which is designed to respond just with punishment to do nothing else. Custodial settings suffer from the same cultural limitations.

STAND ALONGSIDE LEADERSHIP

In some school processes, children are removed from lessons, 'disciplined' by a colleague further up the hierarchy and allocated a sanction. There is no discussion at all. When the pupil arrives at the next lesson, there has been no resolution and resentment simmers, often boiling over.

What is wrong with someone else dealing with them? It is really hard to improve your behaviour skills if someone else always does the dirty bit. Over time, class teachers become deskilled and over-reliant on pastoral systems that play nanny. They are resource-heavy and empathy-light systems that are designed under the premise that some children matter, others don't. If all you have to do is give one warning and then press the button to have the child removed, then you can be sure that someone is paying for the privilege. The cost, inevitably, lies with the children who don't fit the perfect pupil profile. And there are lots and lots and lots of them. Politicians' reputations are built on this collateral damage; children's lives are ruined by it.

When triage is done right it is the children who feel it most keenly. This note, from a 15-year-old at St Mary's Catholic School in Wallasey, seven weeks into testing a triage system, says everything:

Triage works better than Emmaus [the name for the old removal room] because in triage you get to talk to someone about what's happened and how to resolve the situation. Whereas Emmaus was horrible. You weren't listened to at all and could even get put in there for something you haven't done. Teachers would say they will deal with it but they wouldn't. I think triage gives students time to reflect and talk about what's happened and how to move forward.

Often teachers don't want to simply pass over a child to a higher authority to be 'disciplined' because it doesn't feel like support if you aren't involved.

The most effective way to support a colleague who is struggling with a child's behaviour is to stand alongside them. Having a colleague appear alongside you is a fantastic visible show of support. Although the support appears silent, it is anything but. Aside from the message of unity sent to the child, having another emotionally regulated adult alongside you is infectious. The pressure of the moment is lightened and the atmosphere changes in an instant. Three is most definitely not a crowd in this context but a fast track to a swift resolution.

As a head of year, I would come across colleagues exhausted by the protestations of children who had clearly decided that refusing to pick up the can they had just dropped was a hill worth dying on. 'You can't make me pick that up – cleaners would be out of a job if I did. Do you want unemployment in our community? You're a monster. You have no soul.'

And so on. Just the appearance of a colleague would indicate to the child that the game was up and nine times out of ten they would bend down and put the can in the bin.

As standing alongside becomes more common, the children who are prone to turn any request into a national debate begin to realise that they are playing against a large and determined team. One that has a seemingly endless supply of players prepared to get involved.

There is nothing wrong with coaching as an add-on for the children you are most concerned about, but you might be missing a trick by not engaging every adult and child in a coaching relationship.

Remember:

- Leadership needs to be visible and accessible.

- Standing alongside is often better when it is a silent act.

- Authority is always deferred to the class teacher.

- Walk away without saying goodbye.

- Thank the child casually when you see them later: 'Good choice with the can, Oscar.'

EASTON CE ACADEMY: A SAFE SPACE

Easton CE Academy sits in an incredibly diverse community. It is a fabulous school buzzing with energy. Walking out into the playground there are big groups of children dancing in sync with a video screen, scooters whizzing past, balls flying and children on pogo sticks looking awfully pleased with themselves, as children on pogo sticks always do.

Walking into the renamed 'Calm Room' alongside the head teacher, I was immediately struck by gentle breezy music, fairy lights and actual carpet. Someone had clearly gone to a lot of effort to make the space feel safe. I was introduced to the teacher in charge of the room who was ready to receive children who were over-stepping boundaries in class. She described a recent conversion to restorative practice after 22 years of teaching: 'I read your book, and everything changed in September,' she explained. 'Now we are able to get children calm, ready and returned to classroom learning in less than 30 minutes. Before, they were held in this room for hours.' That the room was empty and it was almost lunchtime spoke volumes, but not nearly as much as the tracking data she showed me that demonstrated the positive impact on the children.

This was another room that had a chequered history. It was formerly a place where children were placed as punishment, staring at walls and too upset to do the work in front of them. She explained how it was now about getting them back to learning, making them feel safe enough to talk and not catastrophising their behaviour so that it poisoned the day.

As we chatted, I realised just how much this meant to her. Her way of working had been transformed and, like most of us who discover we have been doing stuff in the wrong way for years, her words were charged with a hint of regret. When you meet teachers who are late converts they always wish they had converted sooner.

Suddenly the door to the Calm Room burst open and a slightly flustered teacher rushed in: 'There's an unregulated child in the playground I need help with.' He ran out again. As we got up to go and help I said to the head, 'That was brilliant – was the use of the word "unregulated" just for my benefit?' He shook his head. 'No, that's just the language we use now.'

His response made it clear that the new culture and approach to behaviour had been embedded. The school's language was forever changed and the direction of travel set.

RESTRAINT AND HOLDING BACK

Restraint is one of the most risky interventions any adult will make – risky in terms of physical safety and also in terms of your career. Decisions made in an instant can play out in lengthy disciplinary investigations and even in court. We can learn a great deal about proportionality from the decisions made around restraint.

Let's start with the extreme end of the scale. If someone is attacking you with a knife, it might be proportionate to defend yourself with a rolling pin. However, if it was a child with a knife made from chocolate, then a rolling pin would be a drastic overreaction. Stopping a child from running into a busy road by holding their shoulders might be proportionate, but shaking them by the shoulders because they haven't done their homework is less proportionate reaction and more assault.

Restraint can result in serious complications if pupils are bent over, held face down or sat on. It can quickly become life or death. Just try doing up your shoelaces and holding a conversation to experience the feeling of a constricted airway. Now add in the chaos of a crisis situation and being forced to hold that position for five minutes.

Following the tragic deaths in youth custody of Gareth Myatt and Adam Rickwood, I worked on the Restraint Accreditation Board to look at the use of restraint and pain compliance techniques on young people in custody. Drafted in for my understanding of behaviour rather than restraint, I learned a great deal about the bravery of prison officers, the unique culture of prisons, and the difficulty of keeping both inmates and officers safe in an often volatile environment. It is really, really hard. When you have seen an officer attacked in the most brutal of ways, it can feel almost irrelevant how the assailant is restrained and taken away. However, there are rights that are universal despite whatever crime may have been committed. Being able to safely restrain an assailant at the height of violent chaos takes an incredible combination of training, skill and sheer courage. I was pleased to be able to contribute, but these complex issues weighed heavy on my mind.

Three words that must be acted upon during a restraint are 'I can't breathe'. Whatever your training, when you hear those words – whatever the context – you *must* release your hold and ensure that everyone else does too. The death of George Floyd is yet another example of how rotten cultures erode training or best practice. 'You are talking so you must be breathing' is a haunting falsehood that is repeated too often.

No teacher puts their hands on a child because they want to. Restraint is never a punishment, surely, and yet recent revelations from special schools and other settings regarding restraint and seclusion show us that complacency is a dangerous mindset.

Elly Chapple, whose daughter suffered the permanent physical and emotional consequences of repeated restraint in a setting deemed to be 'outstanding' by inspectors, is a huge advocate for change:

> We are talking about people currently in ATUs [alternative treatment units], mental health units, private treatment facilities, residential units, schools, respite facilities, children's homes – in short, anywhere children, young people or adults leave their families to be cared for and supported by others. The law is clear that their rights must be upheld. These rights apply to all human beings regardless of difference.[2]

RESTRAINT AND ADDITIONAL NEEDS

Restraint is a huge issue in special education settings where children may have serious health issues. Not only is there a greater risk of restraint or seclusion being subtle or hidden, but there is also more scope for abuse: locking the wheels of a chair, leaving a door handle out of reach, facing a child against the wall, positioning a table so the child's arms are trapped beneath it and plain old locking children into a room that is half the size of a prison cell. Alongside the restraint that goes undiscovered, there are also the endless stories of children being restrained for five hours at a time in a children's home somewhere. The stories keep coming despite legislation, training and political campaigns. Even, and at times especially, in settings where the power is most unbalanced, the greatest abuses go unreported or unnoticed.

---

2   Elly Chapple, We Need to #FlipTheNarrative on How We Treat Children and Young People 'Who Challenge', *Special Needs Jungle* (24 April 2019). Available at: https://www.specialneedsjungle.com/restrictive-interventions-need-change-way-think.

The recent report conducted by the Challenging Behaviour Foundation and Positive and Active Behaviour Support Scotland, *Reducing Restrictive Intervention of Children and Young People*, demonstrated that significant numbers of pupils within school settings (both mainstream and special schools) were at risk of restraint and seclusion. Some 88% of the 204 respondents to the survey said that their disabled child had experienced physical restraint, with 35% reporting it happening regularly. In addition:

- 571 children had experienced restraint and/or seclusion.

- The youngest child was 2 years old.

- In total, 1,058 restraints and 544 seclusions had taken place.

- 83% of these events hadn't been recorded.

- 478 children had been injured.

- 81% of injuries hadn't been recorded.

- In 570 cases there was no accountability.[3]

Restraint is about safeguarding and needs to be placed firmly within that culture and context. You should only ever put your hands on a child to keep them safe. Restraint does not sit within behaviour practice. It is not at the end of the punishment road or the next step in a disciplinary policy.

Of course, judgements made in the blink of an eye can have long-term consequences, but doing nothing may not be an option. However, proportionality is again relevant. Restraint causes genuine internal conflict. I love the idea that no teacher would ever have to restrain a child again, but neither will I stand by and watch a child getting beaten up or a teacher being attacked for a principle. I have been on the inside of too many of these horrible moments to make grand pronouncements about restraint.

There is real nuance here, and real complications, because intervening too late can result in escalation. I was once in a school where staff were

3   Challenging Behaviour Foundation and Positive and Active Behaviour Support Scotland, *Reducing Restrictive Intervention of Children and Young People: Case Study and Survey Results* (January 2019), pp. 3, 20–21. Available at: https://www.challengingbehaviour.org.uk/learning-disability-assets/reducingrestrictiveinterventionofchildrenandyoungpeoplereport.pdf.

trying to talk down a student in the middle of a violent incident, but they were still talking when they needed to act. The student ended up barricaded in a store cupboard, trashing every resource they could get their hands on, with the police on their way. Intervening too quickly can also have its difficulties. You might appear to be over-zealous, too fast to put your hands on a student or too rash. You are between a rocky rock and a very hard place.

A focus on reducing restraint is a healthy course for any setting. 'Rarely restrain' is surely a more reasonable objective in the most fractious settings than restraint elimination – unless someone can explain how releasing your hold on a furious six foot 15-year-old who is about to rip another student apart is the right choice to make. There are victims, and without adults keeping them safe they are not safe.

However, the data is often skewed. One or two children in crisis can cause a spike in restraint that doesn't represent normal practice. The data that is perhaps more concerning is a regular and normalised high number of restraints that pass through a governors' meeting without a raised eyebrow because they are always 'around that number'.

THREE HOLDS

All the evidence around the impact of physical restraint training shows that the holds you have learned, if not used regularly, are all but forgotten within three months and would be dangerous if applied incorrectly. Of course, that is not a great message to give to those buying in training: it makes refresher courses an expensive business. The converse is not great either. The worry is that newly trained colleagues go out and find any excuse to 'practise' on unsuspecting children. 'Mr Harris, Mr Harris, I only asked for a pen – those leg straps are proper overkill.' Incidents of restraint often increase in the week after a training course.

Three simple holds gives those who volunteer to deal with restraint incidents the best chance of staying safe. In a special school setting it might be that everyone needs to be trained in physical holds, while in a mainstream school it is more sensible to have a small group trained to a high standard rather than everyone trained a bit.

Some courses teach more than 30 different holds. By the end of the training I have forgotten most of them, and by the following morning I am probably unsafe. Keeping it simple might mean not using hold number 23 for situation number 6, but you were never going to remember that anyway. Three holds executed consistently and safely are all that is needed. It means that training has the best chance of being implemented accurately.

Of course, the problem with even just three holds is that they rely on physical strength and ability. This is not something that any company selling training will want to admit readily, but it is the inconvenient truth – regardless of the veracity of the techniques. You might be trained to the highest restraint ninja master level, but if you are five foot two and ten stone in weight and the 15-year-old you are trying to restrain is six foot two and seventeen stone, it isn't going to fly. The reality of working in settings where young people are severely traumatised and/or living a deeply violent existence is that when the fighting starts, being fit, strong and built like a small truck can really help. It is no coincidence that in nearly every school for excluded children there are some physically dominant adults. Experience also helps, but keeping everyone safe often means doing everything you can to bring the violence to an abrupt halt.

Similarly, restraint training programmes ignore the problems if the sizes and weights are swapped around. Restraining young children can be even more complicated because they are fragile and the physical dominance of the adult is more pronounced. Everything is harder to judge. Techniques that worked in training on similar sized adults now seem inappropriate when applied to a 7-year-old who is as easy to hold in your hands as jelly on a warm day. Again, little mention is made of applying techniques on small children. It is as if training companies don't want to ask the questions for fear of finding out the answer.

REPORTING AND RECORDING

Reporting is time critical and must be completed as soon as possible after the incident. The next morning is not good enough and will mean that things are forgotten or unintentionally distorted. It is also important that colleagues do not complete reports in collaboration, regardless of how innocent the intent. Reporting on restraint incidents is not there to catch out teachers, but to help the organisation learn better practice through each debrief. Write down what happened straight away or record a voice memo on your phone.

What happens after the incident matters too. Nobody is all that keen to pick over the bones of a crisis, especially when the memory is so raw. It often seems easier just to move on and enjoy the calm after the storm, but that ignores the emotional impact on everyone involved. Hard conversations are not a choice. Sometimes learning from one incident immediately prevents a recurrence.

Decisions made about behaviour in the ebb and flow of the school day are not as critical as those made about restraint. You are unlikely to be held accountable for the former in the same way. However, pupils recognise those adults whose default is consistent, logical and proportionate. It is hard not to build a positive relationship with a teacher who is fair.

STOP THAT!

- Remove the assumption of exclusion from your policy and in conversations about behaviour. Every exclusion decision should be free of automatic tariffs.

- Get rid of the fake consistencies – tariffs for behaviour and punishment, exclusions that ignore additional needs, and allowing adults to escalate beyond a reasonable response.

HOW TO LEAD IT

- Support heads of faculty/area/department need to cultivate a 'buck stops here' approach.

- The road is difficult but it is the right way if it fits your values. Openly accept that we don't have simple solutions to the most complex problems. Explain.

NUGGETS

- Class teachers will have to do less admin work but more conversations with pupils about their behaviour and learning

- Pastoral leads should pick up repeated removals.

- Communication, particularly between the senior leadership team (SLT) and class teachers, needs to be better than ever.

- Don't just post the classroom support plan all over the classroom: make sure the children can verbalise it.

He plods along with satisfactory effort but no great enthusiasm.

Paul Dix, school report, age 13

Chapter 4

RESTORATIVE PRACTICE, KINDNESS AND SOFT POWER

You cannot backfill emotional currency. The time to build a relationship is not when sanctions stop having an impact.

Restorative follow-up is tougher than punishment. It is the harder road where moments of learning replace penitence. The simple restorative meeting that emerged in *When the Adults Change, Everything Changes* is only part of the story.

CRAP RESTORATIVE PATCHES

The word 'restorative' is causing some confusion in education and is in danger of being used to defend the worst punitive cultures. 'Of course, our booths/Sunday morning detentions/public humiliations are restorative' is coupled with the inevitable, 'The way we do exclusion is always restorative.' The bastardisation of the terminology spreads a thin veneer over poorly thought-through policy. It is the velvet glove slid over the iron fist. This lip service (at best) is never truly restorative. Restorative conversations don't need the 'or else' hidden behind the curtain. They are not part of a sanctions hierarchy. They cannot be weighted with punishment or have predetermined 'You *will* apologise at the end of this' outcomes.

Nor is restorative practice a patch to cover the embarrassment of high exclusion figures or another step in the travelator to exclusion. 'We did the restorative thing – didn't work.' It is so much more than conversations between adults and children about poor behaviour. Restorative practice is about the way you respond to the children, how you model routes through arguments/disagreements and the language you use. Restorative practice is not, as Mark Finnis from L30 Relational Systems says, done 'to' the children but 'with' them.[1] That requires sustained behavioural change from the adults.

THE RESTORATIVE, REFLECTIVE LESSON

The daily impact of restorative teaching cannot be underestimated. How you respond in the moment is as important a restorative intervention as any.

Disagreements between children left unsupported can take away the focus on learning very quickly. In classrooms where disagreements/flare-ups/armed skirmishes are common, you need a process that is visible, agreed and always implemented. Delay, divert and dive into the work is particularly useful if you are teaching after morning break or lunch when arguments, born in the playground, burst through the door of your classroom.

1. Delay. Now is not the time – learning time is too valuable – but there might be time at the end of the lesson/at a convenient hiatus/ at the end of the day (by which point they may well be best of friends again anyway).

2. Divert. Separate the children for the lesson/session so they have space to think about other things – that is, space to be distracted by others or space so you can get to them should it spark off again.

3. Dive into the work. Don't allow their behaviour to be the talk of your lesson. Keep the work as the focus and submerge the bickering by learning about something far more interesting.

The pursuit of a reasonable outcome with a logical process is so much better than a hot search for blame at the door of the classroom.

---

1 Mark Finnis, *Independent Thinking on Restorative Practice: Building Relationships, Improving Behaviour and Creating Stronger Communities* (Carmarthen: Independent Thinking Press, 2021).

RESTORATIVE TAKE-UP TIME

Take-up time refers to the time you give a pupil after you have redrawn the boundary. The two minutes gives them the opportunity to reflect on what has happened and make a choice about the next step. It can also take the attention of their peers away from the difficult moment with the teacher, allow them a harrumph and an 'Ain't nothing, fam.' It is a pressure valve that takes the rising steam out of resetting the boundary. When you return to check on progress, your intervention will be cautiously restorative: 'That looks so much better, thank you.' 'You can get there – let me help.' 'Thanks for working with me.'

Take-up time is focused on the child but it is also an opportunity for the adult. The build-up of frustration within a lesson can tempt any of us to forgo take-up time and express our impatience with the child rapidly. The temptation to keep an eye on them and watch their every move is overwhelming. After all, you have just delivered the finest warning with beautiful aplomb and he still appears to be engaged in flicking paint/ flicking Charlie's face/flicking the V's like Billy Casper. I have observed some teachers hovering over the pupil waiting for their behaviour to change, others at the opposite side of the room with virtual binoculars waiting to pounce and a few with X-ray vision watching from the store cupboard. None of it helps. It only increases the emotional pressure on the child.

Use the take-up time that you give the child to reset yourself, and perhaps try a different approach if you need to return. It is easy to set off on the first of a series of steps and feel the blinkers closing in. The positive strategies that began the lesson drift away and the next step on the classroom support plan seems to be the only obvious response. But this is not the time to close off other options; it is exactly the moment to change the rhythm, the tone and the music.

In a truly restorative intervention, the way you return to the pupil may be very different to the way you left them. Focus on the positive moves they have made to make a better choice or shift your positive attention back on to the work. Your manner, language and approach are critical here. You control the climate of your lesson, and that is built on each one of these individual interactions rather than grand gestures. Being emotionally agile so that you don't get hooked in to each moment is a great model for the children.

It is difficult to lose the frustration. Yet shifting your emotions is an essential skill for the restorative teacher. The smallest of adjustments in the toughest of moments is where the real impact lies: you can act restoratively even (and especially) when things get tricky. Control your ego, act with humility and, despite the white noise coming from the child, focus on making the next step the right one for everyone. It is too easy to slip into autopilot and allow the child to rack up the negatives. It is your behaviour that can change the mood, divert the attention or reconnect the child with their positive conduct.

RESTORATIVE CONVERSATION REMIX

The restorative conversation has entered the educational lexicon, partly thanks to those who fear it so much but mostly because teachers know that it is the logical route and it works.

The key to successful restorative conversations is the environment. Walk and talk, stack books and talk, clean tables and talk, pick tomatoes from the allotment and talk, clean the lab benches and talk, put up a display together and talk. The restorative conversation is so much easier and more productive if it isn't just two people sitting at a table with one avoiding awkward eye contact.

The restorative questions are for both the adult and the child. The purpose of the restorative conversation is not to build to a climax of apology, rather to get students to look in the mirror and see their behaviour from a different perspective. It is a coaching conversation using a recent incident in sharp focus. There is real learning here: most of the time for the students, sometimes for everyone.

The fear of the restorative conversation is driven by the desire of some adults not to have to 'explain themselves to the child' or 'take any of the blame' or even 'say sorry to a child'. The block is emotional, but it also runs deep in their philosophy that the adult should have unquestioned authority and control. The counterintuitive is at work here. There is so much more authority and – yes, if you must – control on the other side of a restorative conversation.

The deliberate confusion that opponents use when attacking restorative work is to conflate restorative justice with restorative work or relational practice. Restorative justice is a process used within the criminal justice system between victims and perpetrators. It is careful, sometimes slow and is no quick fix. Restorative work in schools is different. It is more of a parenting conversation – short, predictable and never overwhelming. It does not mirror the process used in custodial rehabilitation. If it did, restorative conversations would take days, not minutes.

Some schools use a slower and more considered process to repair damage between students after particularly nasty incidents but these are the exceptions to the rule. Restorative practice holds up a difficult mirror for poor behaviour. It takes longer at first than dishing out a bucket of punishment, but if done well it simultaneously eases workload and improves relationships.

ALTERNATIVE RESTORATIVE QUESTIONS

A restorative conversation isn't just about those five [restorative] questions for me. The danger is children pay lip service to them. If you know your pupils well you know when this is happening. Lip service is always the enemy of commitment in any conversation.

MARK FINNIS[2]

In my experience, when children are asked the same five questions again and again they develop stock responses which they use for each teacher. They have learned to play the game to avoid taking any real responsibility for their actions. All of the tricks are there: suitably sorrowful eyes, a well-rehearsed list of people 'I have caused problems for', a slick and pre-emptive apology delivered with an appropriate shortness of breath. When you recognise this is happening, it is probably a good idea to

2   Personal correspondence.

broaden the range of questions and keep them on their toes. The first eight questions to make a set of five from were:

1. What happened?

2. What were you thinking at the time?

3. What have you thought since?

4. How did this make people feel?

5. Who has been affected?

6. How have they been affected?

7. What should we do to put things right?

8. How can we do things differently in the future?

Now consider mixing in:

9. What was unusual about today's lesson?

10. Why do you think things went wrong?

11. What would make it easier for us to work together?

12. What would make the next lesson go really well?

13. Where do we go from here?

14. Who could help us with the next steps?

15. If you had the lesson again what would you change?

Mixing in new questions stops some children from gaming the system by giving pre-prepared answers. Others may rely on knowing what to expect, so firing new questions at these children might make them shut down. Think about the child and what will work for them. Make a decision about the number of questions and which ones based on the needs of the child.

It is easy to label a conversation restorative, but much harder to gently interrogate a child about an incident and persuade them to be honest about their emotions. Of course, the fact that you are the adult, you ask the questions and you get to decide on where and how long the meeting takes place has already established a hierarchy. Adults need to find ways to ease that tension. There is a deeper restorative level to be reached, but only if the adult wants it and the relationship allows it.

RESTORATIVE PRACTICE IS A DIFFICULT RETROFIT

It is worth saying in bold block capitals: **DON'T START A BEHAVIOUR REVOLUTION BY THROWING OUT YOUR CONSEQUENCES AND REPLACING THEM ALL WITH RESTORATIVE CONVERSATIONS.** This is not the way to start. Restorative conversations might be the last thing to implement; they are definitely not the first. There is nothing restorative about a conversation with an adult who hasn't yet got to grips with a recognition board or meet and greet and can only read the questions off a card. It is worth noting that children who have previously experienced authoritarian adults will not take easily to an overnight transformation. 'You alright, Miss – only yesterday you was flat-out crazy and now you is offering biscuits?'

There is a good reason why the five pillars of practice – consistent, calm, adult behaviour; first attention for best conduct; relentless routines; scripting difficult interventions; and restorative follow-up – are ordered with restorative follow-up as the final pillar. Children need time to change; adults need even longer, particularly those who have trained and taught using a different mindset. Restorative conversations must be built on a foundation of relational practice. They should be introduced so that adults have a choice about when to use them, with whom and in what circumstances. Blanket policies that allow for nothing else can cause a great deal of unnecessary angst. Shifts in practice must support adults to change, not force them into crisis and see what happens.

Our perception of events constantly lets us down. This is why we need to be slow to judge and why our default mode must be kindness. Just listen to a talk radio station and follow the accompanying social media coverage live and you might believe that each commentator was hearing a different broadcast. When an adult and child try to recount the same incident, perception lets everyone down again. What is remembered – language, context, poignant moments – is recalled with different emphasis and emotion. Anger can cloud the memory, but so does time, age and a thousand other subsequent interactions in school before you get to address what has happened.

HUGS FOR LUNCH

There are people whose social media voice is so compelling that when they say 'come and see us' you know you must. Pitteuchar East Primary School in Fife, like so many great schools, is nothing special from the outside. Head teacher Jennifer Knussen frames her values perfectly: 'It's all about the bairns [children].' And it is.

We spent the morning touring the school deep in excellent conversation. I listened and learned and quickly realised that the voice behind the social media account was even better in real life. There is no focus on punishment, but there are conversations, space to cool off and curiosity from all the adults. There are relationships that visibly flourish between adults and children. Nowhere is this more evident than at lunchtime.

Walking into a buzzing dining room full of hungry children sees any school at its most frenetic. I grabbed a tray and some lunch (there is a special kind of taste to primary school food that is uniquely British) and sat down next to Jen expecting more conversation. As I lifted a fork of mashed potato (from a perfect half sphere), I noticed a line of children queuing up next to our table. I immediately assumed that they were waiting to be told to go to lunch, to show her their work or maybe to apologise for some misdemeanour, but I couldn't have been more wrong.

They waited quietly and patiently for us to get settled and then, one by one, silently approached Jen and gave her a 'side on while eating' hug. Each hug lasted just a few seconds and then the next child would take their place. When I asked Jen about it, she shrugged it off with a joke about how she has a messy top after each lunch hour, but it deserves more than that. The love and respect shown by each child was genuine. They wanted to connect with her physically, appropriately and on their own terms. It was the best lunch I have ever had, and I couldn't even tell you what I ate.

Nurture isn't just a room, it is a culture. Jen is not the only teacher who nurtures. Her example means she is surrounded by adults who do the same. Pitteuchar East is in an area of high deprivation and many children need support with their behaviour. There are incidents – not every day will be perfect – but a culture of nurture means that their behaviour is met with compassion, never anger. Children who need a break/to get angry/to lose control know where to go to get help, calm down and regulate their behaviour.

Nobody who meets Jen and her team would ever mistake kindness for weakness. There is a steely determination behind the hugs that means nobody is ever in doubt about the need for the highest expectations. That certainty and confidence translates into every child feeling safe. Every child knows that it is all about them.

Belonging doesn't get any better than that.

PARENTS AND RESTORATIVE PRACTICE

You need to take the parents with you if you are shifting towards more frequent use of restorative approaches. Lots of parents favour punishment: it is simple, it appears to work and it doesn't demand much thinking time (and 'It never did me any harm' – apart from publicly supporting assault on children). When it becomes clear that school or classroom policy is moving away from punishment as an instant response, they worry. They worry that their children are unsafe, that bad behaviour might go unpunished and that, frankly, you are a sandal-munching, *Guardian*-licking, free love idealist who is experimenting with their punishment-acclimatised child. Sometimes the parents will be your toughest nut to crack, particularly those who would formerly rely on you to discipline their children for them. One head teacher messaged me to say:

We have battled our way to a healthier culture. Some staff have moved on as they want children to be punished and some parents have demanded their child have detentions because they can't get them to do their homework. It's been an interesting journey in all three schools. Relentless routines are going to be key to keeping everyone safe!

Relational practice is evidence based practice, but that doesn't make the conversation with Luke's dad any easier when you explain that you have dealt with the fracas but there is no kicking him out/public flogging/pound of flesh.

Positive communication with parents/guardians is critical, so try the following:

- Involve parents in questionnaires, focus groups, working parties and decision-making.

- Share anonymised examples of successful restorative conversations with parents to show them how behaviour is changed, not just contained.

- Send home the one-page behaviour blueprint with notes to explain the thinking behind it.

- Create a video 'explainer' to send to parents that addresses common concerns.

- Reassure everyone that there are limits to restorative interventions, that victims of violence have a right to feel safe and that not every incident needs a restorative meeting.

RESTORING RABBITS

I wasn't looking forward to the trip to Twycross Zoo. Having been on many disastrous field trips, including the London theatre trip ('Where is their fucking teacher?')[3] and the Alton Towers trip ('I don't care if we are 100 miles from school, just leave him here and we can all go home'), I was wary. Even more so now that I had been promoted to head of year and was the most senior member of staff on duty. This was a big responsibility that nobody wanted. It meant that your head would be on the block when, not if, it all went very, very badly wrong. None of this was helping me to stay calm.

---

3   See Paul Dix, 'Are We Going on the Tub?' In Ian Gilbert (ed.), *The Working Class: Poverty, Education and Alternative Voices* (Carmarthen: Independent Thinking Press, 2018), pp. 95–98.

However, I was determined that this time it would go without a hitch. We loaded the children onto the coach, slightly disappointed that everyone had turned up (the worst behaved children often seem to have the best attendance records). No matter, we had a game plan: children cunningly divided into groups, big characters separated, strong colleagues deployed strategically. It worked like a dream. Sunny day, everyone happy. As I checked the children back onto the coach, I was surprised that they were on time and suitably exhausted from chasing penguins/ antagonising lions/over-petting lambs.

On the way back I allowed myself a small inner smile. This would be a field trip that would serve as an example to those who came after: immaculate behaviour, actual learning, nobody died. On my way home from school in the car, I may even have played a little Manilow: 'Could It Be Magic'.

When the phone rang at 7pm, the magic died and the emotions began to overwhelm. It was Sue, a colleague: 'Paul, the zoo has been on the phone. A rabbit is missing.' Four words I didn't want to hear.

At times during the day I had been reminded of the play *Our Day Out* by Willy Russell: chaos on the bus, mild shoplifting and animal kidnapping. I had now broken the fourth wall and entered the drama. However, in the play the animals are retrieved by the zookeeper before the children get onto the bus to leave. I had not been as vigilant. In fact, the child with the 'bunny up the jumper' had paused to chat to me at some length before boarding.

Predicting a difficult conversation with the head the next morning, Sue managed to find the rabbit, explain to the parent that it had not been 'found in the park' and was, in fact, the property of Twycross. I resolved not to be in charge of trips again. At least until the next time.

The restorative path is rarely the easiest one to walk. Holding up a mirror for children to see how their behaviour looks requires skill, empathy and practice. Sometimes it doesn't go well, is awkward and doesn't lead to where you thought it would. It is not a panacea for behaviour but it teaches so much more than 'no'. A good restorative conversation builds connection and leaves everyone understanding where the boundaries lie. As your behaviour policy and practice matures, the hard work and commitment to restorative conversations builds relational capital that beats pure punishment every time.

STOP THAT!

- Forcing colleagues to lead restorative conversations before they have grasped the shift in adult behaviour that is needed.

- Referring to restorative conversations in public: 'Now Misha, when we talked yesterday you promised to …'

- Don't threaten punishment to try and bring a crisis to a halt.

HOW TO LEAD IT

- How you treat your colleagues is central to leading the momentum of kindness. Your use of subtle (and often private) positive recognition for adults makes it easier for them to be drawn into the same recognition for their pupils.

- Be overheard often using the restorative questions and intervening with restorative language.

- Monitor the numbers of restorative meetings. It will be natural for some colleagues to have fewer restorative meetings than others. Look to support colleagues who, given the choice between a consequence or a restorative conversation, always choose the former.

- Deal with misconceptions about restorative work. Restorative conversations are not an opportunity for children to negotiate the boundaries. In fact, restorative conversations rely on accountability, high expectations, limit setting with support, safety and care. Understanding and teaching boundaries is an essential part of teaching. At the end of the conversation, the boundaries remain the same whether the child agrees with them or not. There is no break with the consistent agreement. Values and rules are used to frame conversations; they are not thrown on the table as a prelude to a Mexican stand-off.

NUGGETS

- Leaving a chocolate bar in a pigeon hole is perhaps the simplest and most impactful of all kindnesses.

- Walking into a room and taking over the class for five minutes can sometimes give a colleague the breathing space they need to speak to a child/make a cup of tea/scream in the cupboard.

- Humility is always the best vantage point for a truly restorative conversation.

An unruly class member who, even when he tries, does not usually produce good enough work on time. A 'natural' actor.

Paul Dix, school report, age 12

Chapter 5

COACHING IN THE RAIN

One more for the Gipper.

After the adults change, the systems need to change. For the systems to change, the timetable needs to make room for coaching. Rita Pierson's excellent provocation that 'Every kid needs a champion' cannot be left to chance.[1] For every child to have a champion, some system redesign will be required. Coaching for all students is an essential retrofit for your classroom and your school. If you need to lose assemblies, move the start of the school day or even reclaim some curriculum time (I feel your rage, science teachers) – it will be worth the struggle. With younger children being taught as one class, you may have to be creative and question things that could be flexible: circle time, the personal, social and health education curriculum and afterschool coaching clubs.

POLICY AND PRACTICE

In many schools, the amount of pastoral contact time has been reduced to a bare minimum. I remember a particularly indignant inspector who demanded that children be taught during morning tutor time. He was incredulous that we would have conversations, check in with the students and talk about the day ahead. It was apparently 'wasted time'. The school duly imposed more structured 'tutor time PowerPoints' and the children who needed the regulation of a calm adult first thing in the morning struggled every day. What a plonker.

---

1   Rita Pierson, Every Kid Needs a Champion, *TED.com* [video] (May 2013). Available at: https://www.ted.com/talks/rita_pierson_every_kid_needs_a_champion?language=en.

Not everything can be taught through the formal curriculum. Squeezing every ounce out of pastoral time is not just mean or small-minded; it changes the nature of the education provided. It reduces the support for those most in need and for every child who is usually perfectly well self-regulated but is just having a bad day. The children learned nothing from their daily diet of dull, enforced PowerPoints, apart from understanding that the adults seemed to care more about the whining of a weasely inspector than about them.

The first half hour of the day is critical for children who come through chaos to get to school. They need to regulate through first contact with emotionally contagious adults. This is so important in schools for excluded children that without it nobody would be able to teach anything in lesson one. In other schools, the children who most need that connection find themselves in isolation rooms less than five minutes after the start of the first lesson.

In great coaching cultures, it is not just the adults whose emotional stability is contagious but the model provided by the other students. There is group regulation and support. A well-managed, vertically structured group means that schools with coaching at the heart of pastoral support are not just trying to keep their students on track academically, they are also helping to keep them mentally, physically and emotionally on track.

Teachers are no different. They are much happier when surrounded by emotionally regulated adults. If you walk into work and a colleague is violently attacking the photocopier – tears streaming down their face and a crotch full of ink powder – it can affect you. If someone brings you a coffee and a Walnut Whip, the first lesson looks like a good lesson already.

EVERY CHILD GETS COACHING

Carr Manor Community School near Chapeltown in Leeds is an all-through (4–19 years) school with 1,336 pupils, 54% of who qualify for free school meals and 42% receive special educational needs and disabilities (SEND) support. Some 43% of pupils live in the 10% most deprived postcodes.

It is perhaps not the easiest place to choose to build a school based on relational, restorative and coaching principles. There are other schools in other places that would provide more readily fertile ground for such an innovation – maybe a rural school with high rates of literacy or an international school with behaviour that is already exemplary. In other cities and in other places, people might look at the relative wealth of the surrounding community and demand a strict punishment rich approach to beat the disadvantaged into line. However, the community that Carr Manor serves gets so much better than that.

At the core of Carr Manor's model are vertically structured coaching groups (circles) of between eight and ten pupils who meet three times a week with their coach. The structure is 'Check In', 'Check Up' and 'Check Out'. They get together on a Monday morning to check in, refocus after the weekend, co-plan for the week ahead and anticipate any bumps in the road. On Wednesday afternoons they meet again to check up on progress, deal with outstanding issues and complete structured tasks. Sometimes Wednesdays will be 'Coaching Plus' days when coaching groups join up and work collaboratively. The coaching groups meet again on Friday afternoons to review the week, look ahead to the next week and check out for the weekend.

The coaching model is relational and focused on pro-social skills development. The pupils are given an opportunity to talk to and listen to others in self-supporting groups. In their research into restorative practice in schools, Jo Warin and Rebecca Hibbin have found that 'the deliberate promotion of exposure to diversity within these vertically structured Coaching Groups provided pupils with pro-social learning opportunities that were likely to be largely unavailable in a traditional school and social groupings'.[2]

Coaches are trained to offer one-to-one support, ensuring that each child has a 'partner in learning' to provide ongoing care and encouragement. An additional benefit is the relationships that develop

---

2   Jo Warin and Rebecca Hibbin, *Embedding Restorative Practice in Schools* (March 2020), p. 10. Available at: https://www.researchgate.net/publication/341215702_EMBEDDING_RESTORATIVE_PRACTICE_IN_SCHOOLS.

between pupils of all year groups who meet in coaching groups and then act as a peer support network for each other around school.

This was evidenced in a short inspection report from 2018 which stated:

> The school's coaching programme is a major strength of the school. The impact of this programme on relationships between staff and pupils and the inclusive ethos of the school are impressive. Almost all staff are coaches and they know the children in their coaching groups very well. The system of weekly checking in, checking up and checking out ensures that staff are able to identify any concerns early and take actions swiftly.[3]

The depth of coaching experience in the school and the utter commitment of all adults to follow a restorative path is palpable. Here, experience and talent is valued and nurtured. They employ ex-pupils who, as adults, are often reminded of their less responsible contributions to school life in days gone by. Yes, there is laughter and people are relaxed, but there are still difficult days and tricky situations. However, the entire school community knows in its bones that it is doing the right thing, not the easy thing.

Even asking the pupils randomly in the corridor elicits unexpected responses, even from the 'cool' kids: 'We love it here. The teachers are great and we all get along really well.' I ask another child in case the first was a plant. I receive the same unerringly positive response. Even a child pulled out of a coaching session looks slightly irritated to be missing the learning. On the surface, Carr Manor is a thoroughly excellent school. It is when you scratch the surface that you realise it is also truly remarkable.

In January 2020, we put on a Lose the Booths live event in partnership with Carr Manor, so I know from personal experience the commitment of every adult in every role at the school, the children, the philosophy and the mission. It is the sort of place that would make you want to move house just to have your own children educated there. Politicians, the great and the good all visit and shower

---

3   Ofsted, Short Inspection of Carr Manor Community School (9 July 2018), p. 2. Available at: https://files.ofsted.gov.uk/v1/file/2786537.

plaudits on Carr Manor and then leave again. What we all need to do is learn from their success and promote it nationally to show other schools what is possible.

Carr Manor's exclusion data is no magic trick. *Zero permanent exclusions since 2005 and fewer than 14 fixed-term exclusions each year since 2014.* It is evidence of the right culture, great relational practice and what happens after the adults change. Nor is it some outlier at the edge of the system. Zero excluding or rare excluding schools are commonplace – a fact that undermines all of the arguments for zero tolerance regimes where they believe that 'a little bit of oppression/exclusion/darkened booth goes a long way'. These schools are an inconvenient truth among proponents of punishment rich schools. Behaviour is, again, politics.

> The capacity the coaching model provides across the school and its impact makes it a golden thread that self-sustains. Ownership of coaching lies with the whole community – it is a genuine 'with' approach to building capacity, expectations and performance. A restorative approach to challenge and full support.
>
> **SIMON FLOWERS, EXECUTIVE HEAD TEACHER, CARR MANOR COMMUNITY SCHOOL**

TEACHABLE MOMENTS IN CHAOS

In the heart of a behaviour crisis, coaching might seem like bringing a banana to a gunfight. In fact, it might be the perfect moment for bananas.

In sport, coaching is there in times of joy and crisis. When things get tough, the coach doesn't hide away. When the rain comes they get wet too. They remind the athlete of their training, their routines and, critically, link their discipline in the most emotionally charged moments to their desired future success. It is a simple link that is affirming, not critical. The interruption might reference prior agreements or targets, but is very much about the present. 'This is the steep bit of the path you want to walk.' 'I know it's hard now but it will be worth it when we can share this with mum.' 'Fame costs and here's where you start paying … in sweat' (to quote Lydia Grant).

We often back away to give pupils more time and space during a crisis, particularly if we have no relationship or emotional currency with the child. However, a coach or teacher with a tankful of emotional currency may be able to step forward rather than back, to recognise the teachable moment and grab it before it passes. Coaching designed into the heart of your work with pupils gives them the right support when things get rough.

There are even some teachable moments that are best taken advantage of in the heat of distress. Timing is everything: the adults must have changed because threats and punishment will wreck the opportunity.

Redthread, an organisation working to reduce knife crime, have coaches stationed in the A&E departments of some Central London hospitals. They are searching for the teachable moment. When someone arrives with stab wounds they are ready to try and intervene emotionally not long after the medical team has intervened physically:

> When someone is critically injured, they are suddenly removed from the streets. They are dependent on doctors for their survival. They may be in pain. The aim is to teach them that this is a moment they should grasp. A junction in their lives where a choice can be made. To go back, or to move on.[4]

When the patient is away from other influences, there might be a space to talk. When they are just the other side of a life-threatening experience, they might be open to thinking about a different pathway.

Less dramatic moments, but no less teachable, happen in schools every day. Too many adults try to teach during an escalating confrontation, so by the time the teachable moment comes they have walked away or become immersed in the fog of the argument. Trying to teach, and making things worse, is a common mistake for parents as well as teachers. 'If you don't put that down right now it will burn you … Oh, see … Screaming won't help … Why didn't you listen? … Why are you hopping around?' The teachable moment might come after the first signs of regret when the tears have subsided or it might be the following morning when everything seems possible again. It will almost certainly be when the chaos has abated, not as it is gaining momentum.

A coaching conversation with a child who is calming down often starts with, 'I am here when you are ready to talk.' This conversation is one for the here and now. It doesn't deal with those hardy perennials such as, 'What do you think mum would say?' or the big questions of life, 'What do you want to be when you are older?' or, indeed, open the vault of punishment, 'If you carry on like this I will have no option but to …'

What you say to the most distressed children at the point of crisis really matters. This isn't a time for instant judgement or a sceptical tone. It is a time to carefully consider your intervention while also weighing up whether silence might be a better response for a while longer. I asked

---

4   Tom Symonds, The Non-Medics in A&E Fighting the Effects of Knife Crime, *BBC News* (3 November 2017). Available at: https://www.bbc.co.uk/news/uk-41818289.

an audience of 50 expert teachers who work with the most distressed learners to suggest what words work best for them most often. Here are their 50 suggestions.

It's OK, I've got you. It'll be OK ...	I remember the other day when you ... It was incredible.
I'm here for you.	How can we sort this out together?
It's OK to feel this way. Let's talk more about it and put a plan together.	I see you. You matter.
How about we go outside and talk for a bit?	You have so much to contribute. I really appreciate you being here.
I believe in you.	What happened?
You can turn this around.	I'm sorry you're upset. When you're ready, let me know what's going on and I will help you.
You're doing amazingly. I see your efforts.	I'm not going to say I know exactly how you feel. I will say that you are allowed to feel how you feel, and I'm here if you want to talk about it.
I care.	I'm listening.
Tell me your worries. Let me help you get to the other side.	Tears are OK. I'm comfortable with tears.
Let's break it down into small steps.	Regulate with a walk or practical activity, then come back to the situation when you're ready.

How's it going – fancy a walk?	Tell me more about what's going on. Help me to understand.
I've noticed you are struggling today. How can I help?	What can I do to help you right now?
You talk. I'll listen.	It's OK. Come and talk to me when you're ready.
Let's put the kettle on.	We're here when you're ready.
Take some time – I'm here when you're ready to talk.	Can you tell me a bit more? Then we can work it out together.
You're stronger than you know. You've got this.	I can tell you're not feeling it today. What can I do to help you?
I can see that you're struggling and I'm proud of you for pushing through this.	Whatever you're feeling right now, it's OK. Setbacks are temporary but you will remain. And you're capable of anything.
What would you like to see happen now?	How could we overcome this?
Take your time, take a breath and tell me one small thing that is bothering you.	[Touch on the shoulder] Are you OK?
What's been on your mind?	That sounds really hard. I'm here to listen if you want to talk about it.
I'm listening – what can I do to help?	How can we get through this?

I'm here if you want to talk.	Are you ready to share with me how you're feeling?
I'm here to help.	What's going on? [wait, readjust, listen]
I know you can do this.	How can I make it better for you?
You're always welcome here and have a safe place.	I'm really glad you're here.

Internal coaching between adults and between adults and children is an excellent foundation for improving relationships, understanding and resilience. For the most entrenched behaviours, it might be that an outside view is valuable. If you are wondering what more you can do, then the step you might be overlooking is outreach.

OUTREACH COACHING HEROES

Outreach is the stage before exclusion that is often missing. Some of the best coaching work goes completely unnoticed because outreach doesn't have a classroom, desks or even a building. However, there is nothing more powerful than a great outreach team. Working discreetly behind the scenes and alongside class teachers, they are skilled at managing more than just the children.

Entering a classroom where a teacher is facing high levels of distressed behaviour from a pupil every day is a complicated business. The child certainly doesn't want to see the teacher, but it is not uncommon for the teacher to feel a similar frustration. This is often an emotional and anxious situation that will have a lot of history.

The need to build relationships with both the adult and the child has real urgency if any intervention is to be effective. Outreach teachers dive into sometimes very chaotic and emotionally unstable classes, often in environments where there are more issues than just one child. They prevent situations from escalating, train teachers in the moment and connect with children with incredible skill.

Outreach is often the most effective intervention for children at risk of exclusion, but it is also a service that is easy to cut when the bean counters arrive. Successful outreach work should be invested in and celebrated because every pound is paid back a thousand fold. The emotional cost is also reduced as children, parents and teachers avoid the wrench of moving to a specialist school, with all of the complications and sense of failure that entails.

Ruth Browne from the Golborne Education Centre in London (part of TBAP) has lots of experience and deep knowledge in this area. Their outreach team work with some of the most complicated children in the capital, they give children and teachers the coaching they need when they need it, and they support children who would have been permanently excluded to become successful where they are. Most brilliantly of all, the outreach team does this without compromising the teacher–pupil relationship, allowing the support to fade away seamlessly. Ruth Browne says:

Our outreach team provides support to 38 primary schools and their learners. They work at the whole school, class and individual level. With clear criteria for referral involving school teachers and SENDCo, the team use a clear behaviour framework and an integrated approach to help teachers understand behaviour, clarify their concerns and plan for change. Feedback from schools who access the service is outstanding.[5]

SIMPLE, CURIOUS COACHING

Good coaching should be available for every adult working with children. Coaching makes performance management systems look expensive, distracting and ineffective.

The simplest way to do this is to enable staff to work in small groups and coach each other. Without the pressure of reporting to the hierarchy, coaching groups can thrive. Agreements within the groups are important, so taking time to talk though the process is critical. However, his initial investment of time pays off because self-supporting groups just try to get better at their work. Keeping it simple with groups of three or four means that colleagues are not overloaded by coaching others or with feedback for themselves. It also means that when groups meet every couple of weeks, the cakes/biscuits/Prosecco don't have to be shared with too many others.

Coaching triads seek to improve practice from each person's starting point, so make sure everyone is working with colleagues with whom they can be open and honest. Trust makes coaching work. If you have to spend the next three months building a relationship with someone in your group, then nothing will change quickly. Being forced to be in a coaching group with someone you don't trust is as welcome as a seating plan on a training day.

Targets for improvement are set by individuals and supported by the group, not imposed from above. Coaching groups are ideally placed to

5   Personal correspondence.

support with research. Free from accountability, there are no limits on their ability to innovate practice.

SETTING UP A COACHING GROUP

There are four key steps when establishing your coaching groups:

1. AGREE THE BOUNDARIES

The purpose of a coaching group is to help each member to improve their practice on their own terms and from their own starting point. Ask each group to discuss the following points and to negotiate the boundaries for their own group:

- Coaching is a no-blame environment and needs to be solution focused. How can we make this happen?

- Nothing is repeated, reported or shared outside the group. Can we agree that from this point onwards?

- Weekly check-in and fortnightly meeting time needs to be agreed and kept free. What are going to be the best times for our group?

- You can change your group without drama whenever you want. Shall we agree how to make this as easy as possible?

2. HOW TO WORK IN COACHING GROUPS

The coaching groups now need to decide if they will support one another through lesson observation, team teaching, co-planning, lesson recording and discussion, online learning, earpiece coaching, testing strategies for specific children, professional development/training or just by talking and reflecting regularly together.

It is important for groups to establish how they would like to be coached. Do they want a pure coaching model where the coach questions, actively listens, challenges and draws out the answers, or a more instructional model that blends questions with motivation and guidance (rather like the role of a sports coach)? The two variants have a different pace and rhythm. The latter needs more planning and perhaps different groupings, so that expert teachers coach less experienced colleagues. The former has less impact on workload but, depending on groupings, may be slower to progress.

Groups should be free of any pressure to record their progress on performance management grids or professional development record. Creeping accountability taints the process and will erode trust between colleagues.

A good coach is professionally curious. They ask the questions that you need to ask yourself but haven't got round to yet. They tease out the answers and provide the structure to think through to a solution. Just walking and talking and staying curious in your questioning might be enough. Focusing on single challenges also works well. Too much process kills it, so keep it simple and trust in your colleagues.

Just like a good restorative meeting, the best coaching conversations are not held interview-style across a desk. The distraction of a task or the easy rhythm of a walk can make all the difference, particularly when you are getting to know each other better.

3. GETTING STARTED

When the groups have had a chance to talk through the boundaries, their aims and how they will work, set them off discussing the first questions:

- What one thing do you want to get better at?

- How will you know when you have succeeded?

- What is the first step you want to take?

4. SUPPORTING AND RESOURCING COACHING GROUPS

Focus on making it easy for the groups to meet:

- Create a school CPD library with suggestions from each group.

- Earmark protected time for groups to meet fortnightly.

◾ Allow flexibility for groups to observe or team teach as part of their agreed process.

Before the session ends, ask each group to note the next two check-ins and meetings in their diaries for the rest of the term. Nobody needs another WhatsApp group, but this might be one that you allow.

COACHING, GOD WILLING

As a young teacher, I would try to shape my own coaching with pupils so that it was as good as it could be. I had not yet discovered anything that would be recognised as coaching practice. Basically, like most of us, I was making it up as I went along.

Mohammed was going off the rails. You could feel it in his demeanour and see it in his behaviour, which he displayed all over the school. As his form tutor, I had started to pick up the first rumbles. He was never a particularly diligent scholar but Mohammed would normally steer away from confrontation. He was well under the radar and there were much bigger fish to worry about. It started, as it often does, with him being removed from lessons for a variety of legitimate but unusual reasons: saying 'Chester will get you' in response to every request from colleagues, refusing to remove his coat and burying his head into it to hide away, and barking – yes, barking – repeatedly and randomly.

I really liked Mohammed. He was kind and had a depth of character that made him interesting. His dry sense of humour often cut through the mundane. I needed to have a serious conversation with him and summoned up my best serious self to try and coach him through whatever was going on. Although he batted away any notion that there was anything more to it than 'being bored with lessons', it was clear that all was not well. It was something that would take time to reveal itself, but it was time to deal with the present first.

We had an excellent conversation where I subtly whipped out hastily sourced motivational phrases, attempting to shift his attitude and address his poor behaviour. I employed everything I had learned so far and stayed suitably stern throughout. He picked up the tone and answered with humility and respect. It seemed that he was keenly aware of his poor conduct and made every promise to repair and reset.

I may have had a smug moment of self-satisfaction that I was saving the world one child at a time. Perhaps, somewhere in the distance, Whitney Houston was singing the line, 'I believe the children are our future', while a teaching award was being gently polished and engraved with my name. I could feel the optimism and the conversation drew to a close. We ran through our agreement which was practical and achievable.

'Excellent,' I said. 'I know you're going to hit those targets.' 'Yes Sir, inshallah [God willing].' I struggled for a response. 'Yes, Mohammed, inshallah, and you will make every effort to make it happen.' 'No Sir,' he replied kindly and with a slight shrug of the shoulders, and then very definitely, 'Inshallah.'

I still had a lot to learn.

What coaching questions might you pose to your pupils today? Could focusing on solutions even in the trickiest of moments teach us something? Choose from:

- Who could you ask for help?

- What do you need in order to get back to work?

- How can we move forward from here?

- If you tried that, what do you think might happen?

- Is there anything stopping you from …?

- What would your best version of yourself do next?

- What does success look like?

- Have you tried to solve the problem? How?

- What do you need most right now?

- What is important about that to you?

- Why not?

Try making coaching questions part of your intervention strategy for your pupils. The right one at the right time can develop a difficult conversation into a truly reflective one.

SEND THAT CHILD TO THE HEAD TEACHER FOR SOME SERIOUS COACHING!

Parklands Primary School in Leeds is a remarkable school. In the middle of some of the worst poverty in the UK, it is an utterly inspiring place.

At Parklands, children who are asked to go and see the head teacher because they are struggling with their behaviour feel reassured, not fearful of instant retribution. Expectations for behaviour are not affected by this certainty. Everyone recognises that if children are finding it difficult to stay within the boundaries, they need support first, not the threat of a higher authority or a large portion of sanction.

Head teacher Chris Dyson has his door open all day and expects children to arrive in his office at any time. Regardless of the perceived importance of other meetings, the children come first. I vividly recall attending a meeting with a very senior politician in his office. The meeting was punctuated by the arrival of children. Most had been sent to share their achievements and came with work to show him. A few who shuffled in had been sent there because they were not coping in lessons. Chris distracted and redirected brilliantly, introducing the children to his visitors and picking out the child's best traits to share.

His private words of reassurance have an incredible impact on the children. Chris has so much emotional currency, so much compassion and such great relationships that even the most angry or upset child melts when he speaks to them. But the children don't come trying to hide their anger or upset. They don't need to put on an act because it isn't a moment of fear or trepidation for them. They know what to expect. Do not confuse his kindness for weakness: standards and expectations could not be higher.

There is so much trust that words don't always need to be spoken in these interactions. Presence, understanding and appropriate touch are all that are needed. Don't be under any illusions, though: Chris and his team are not magicians. The trust-building, lack of fear or shouting, and certainty of response take time and hard work. There are no overnight transformations in education, but there are miracles.

I've recently had a couple of challenging lessons with a pupil.

But next lesson I'll start again.

I'll forgive.

I'll move on.

I'll consider new strategies.

It will be a fresh start.

I won't bear a grudge.

Because I'm the teacher.

And they're still a child.

KAREN KNIGHT, HISTORY TEACHER

STOP THAT!

- Trying to teach or tell children the behaviour you want while they are in crisis.

- Forcing adults into coaching triads with which they are uncomfortable. Trust is the most valuable coaching commodity.

HOW TO LEAD IT

Here are five things worth knowing about coaching from Lucie Lakin, executive head teacher at Wetherby High School:

- Don't only do it with some children.

- Do it vertically, not in year groups.

- Include *all* staff. It is an advocate role, not an expert-to-impart-subject-wisdom role.

- Don't steal the time for curriculum stuff so that not everyone is doing it, except the kid who needs maths intervention.

- Don't use it to tick any inspector's box.

NUGGETS

- Teaching children and adults to 'be coachable' is critical. Talk about the roles and responsibilities but, most importantly, be explicit about the behaviours that are needed.

- Use existing pastoral time, form tutor time, assembly time and circle time for coaching opportunities. Make it a priority. I can't imagine that even the best assemblies are more productive than time spent in a well-run coaching group.

An interesting and alert boy, he must still learn not to work just when it pleases him.

Paul Dix, school report, age 12

Chapter 6

EXCLUSION ISN'T A BEHAVIOUR STRATEGY

The child is not for the school. The school is for the child.

The phrase 'exclusion is not a behaviour strategy' seems so obvious that it should be redundant, and I ought to be sent to walk the streets of Sarf London barefoot in my pants for even speaking it. But behaviour is politics, and politics loves doublethink.

Exclusion is a failure. It is not a sign that everything is going smashingly. It is not part of the plan. Neither is it a sign that things will change or the miracle 'short sharp shock' that so many authoritarian politicians want it to be. It is a failure of the system, of resourcing, of individuals and, perhaps, of the support outside the school. Wherever the blame lies, exclusion is a failure.

Of course, the cheerleaders of rising exclusion will tell you they are saving the 'good' children, the idea being that if we don't rain down punishment hard enough on the 'bad' it will ruin the education of everyone else. A bad apple spoiling the barrel seems a long way from 'You belong. We are a community. We look after each other'. I suppose some schools are a bit grumpy.

Encouraging schools to exclude children, while simultaneously and systematically cutting funds from alternative provision, is deeply irresponsible. For some, exclusion is a wonder drug and its side effects can be conveniently ignored. The truth is that more children end up on the streets. The incredulity of those who deny the connection between exclusion and youth crime is just pantomime. It reminds me of the people who used to deny the link between cigarettes and lung cancer with 'They haven't really proven a link yet'.

LAST RESORT APOLOGISTS

'Last resort' is a phrase often used to excuse appallingly disproportionate responses. In every context, one person's last resort is another's second step. Last resort apologists know that claiming 'It was the last resort' will convince their audience of the huge amount of preventative work that has gone in. In reality, it is an excuse to leap to the most extreme response as quickly as possible. The rogue prison officer who uses restraint after he has asked an inmate to go behind the door (i.e. go into his cell). The head teacher under pressure from hyper-accountability measures who excludes faster than before. The angry parent who smacks her child to stop them picking things off the supermarket shelf.

In settings where the last resort is distorted and fixed-term exclusions are high, the climate echoes through every classroom – and not in a good way. After all, if students are being excluded for petty misdemeanours, why shouldn't I send students out of my classroom for even less? The trust between children, their families and the school gets chipped away at by pettiness. Parents who complain about the school's response to behaviour are often concerned about proportionality. Big sticks for small mistakes is not an intelligent, fair or logical response. When harsh approaches are modelled and encouraged by the leadership, the culture of the school becomes contaminated. It results in a 'them' and 'us' narrative that eats away at relationships and community support.

It is one thing to address what happens when a student is sent out of a room, but much harder to dig deeper into lesson removal, establish positive protocols to reduce it and develop a consistent sequence of small steps rather than leaping to the last resort.

Here are seven things to try before removing a child from the classroom (not all at once!):

1. Stand close by or sit alongside them, if everyone is comfortable/ COVID free.

2. Give them a responsibility or a job (not a fool's errand).

3. Positively reinforce good behaviour and reflect back successes.

4. Find a gentle way to change who the child is working with: 'Rumi needs help with …' is usually enough.

5. Use the child's good work as an example for others to reframe them as successful in the task.

6. If they are not disrupting others, give them more time and space to recover their behaviour.

7. Tell them you want them to stay with the lesson, remind them that it matters to you and keep reinforcing the learning culture you want to embed.

The use of tariffs and conveyor belts of hierarchical control and punishment have become ubiquitous in schools in the United States and England. Too many children now reach the end of the belt and fall off – often into a darker side of life. In case you never spent time excluded from school, it is worth knowing that there are a thousand new temptations when you are walking the streets excluded, when almost everyone else is in school. I should know: I tried as many as I could.

FREE PARKING?

One alternative to internal exclusion is parking: relocating a child from your class to another class for the rest of the lesson. When a school has lesson exclusions down to a handful a day, then parking is perfectly manageable. A rota of senior and more experienced teachers accept grumbling students who sit at a pre-prepared desk and continue with their studies.

There are some key principles to making parking work:

■ Children are sent to classes that are not of the same year group. In fact, the bigger the age gap, the more likely it is that the receiving class will not be disrupted.

■ Students are collected from the lesson and escorted to the right place.

- They have work to complete that they understand.

- The teacher receiving the student is confident in doing so. Colleagues who are new to the school or who are still establishing themselves do not receive students.

As a head of faculty, I would always enjoy having 'visitors'. I tried to make sure that the message to the child was not simply 'You have behaved badly'. Moreover, it was an opportunity for them to see the focus and dedication of the older students – how they loved their learning so much that their behaviour was never close to the edge. I often found my own teaching sharpened as we all tried to subtly shift the visitor's expectations. Older students would often take a couple of minutes away from their work to speak to the child in the 'parking space'. They would counsel and mentor them, and even calm them down when necessary. I truly welcomed these moments. You could see the values transferred from teacher to students being remixed and taught from student to student.

With a strong team, parking can also create some sensible checks and balances around removing children from class. You feel the gentle pressure of not sending a child out because you know it will be an imposition on a colleague. The balance here is important. If there is too much pressure not to remove then colleagues may feel they need to hold on to students for too long. Similarly, in a school that is struggling to maintain control and is at the beginning of a behaviour improvement plan, a parking system that delivers too many students to others will end in disaster. 'Err, Mr Dix, half of Year 9 are at the door – should I get the big table out?' A handful of students spread across a handful of teachers is manageable. Mass parking with lots of students being sent to other classes is a sign that your school is not at the right stage for the strategy.

As a classroom teacher fighting to find my feet, the thought of being placed on a parking rota was terrifying. Carefully curated lessons could be destroyed by random arrivals who would enter the room like a footballer raising a trophy. The crowd would roar and the legendary status of certain individuals would soar. It would take me 15 minutes to put the lesson back together again, by which time the momentum had been lost. Done badly or in the wrong context, parking can cause twice the problem it seeks to solve.

Unfortunately, the overuse of parking is often down to resources. If you simply don't have the budget to staff a triage system then parking appears to be the cheaper option. Yet with the risk of so many lessons being wrecked, and the inevitable need to have more corridor patrols, it is a false economy. Worse still, you will find more staff being called to lessons where students have already been parked, which undermines everything.

THE GLASGOW MODEL – CREDIT FOR THE HARD SHIFT

A late friend and colleague, Miller Thompson, fought his whole life to train teachers in Nurture practice. He was one of the early proponents of Nurture groups in Scotland and worked with enormous passion to produce positive change.

The principles of Nurture are:

- Children's learning is understood developmentally.
- The classroom offers a safe base.
- Nurture is important for the development of self-esteem.
- Language is a vital means of communication.
- All behaviour is communication.
- Transitions are significant in children's lives.

A school that has Nurture principles at its core is full of relational practice. The move away from deterrence and punishment cultures is a significant shift. This isn't about just having a Nurture Room; it is about establishing a nurturing climate that responds to behaviour through a very different lens.

Glasgow is the Nurturing City. The Glasgow Model is not a single strategy but has grown and developed through a series of separate initiatives over many years. Its recent branding is testament to the confidence that the city has with its direction of travel. And the evidence is strong that it is the right direction. What is equally incredible is why such excellent practice does not inform and guide the Department for Education in London, Sydney and New York. In Glasgow, there is a recognition that 'these are our children' and that excluding them onto the streets or into poor quality alternative provision is not good enough. The ethos is clear: what is right for your own child must be right for other people's children.

There is also an acceptance of a direct relationship between reducing violence and a focus on Nurture in schools. The Scottish Violence Reduction Unit (SVRU) is a national centre of expertise on violence. Part of Police Scotland, the SVRU targets violence wherever it occurs, whether it is on the streets, in schools or in homes. It works closely with schools and local authorities to manage the most difficult cases, but also to significantly alter the approach to violence and criminality. The unit has adopted a public health perspective by treating violence as an infection that can be cured. The SVRU is the only police member of the World Health Organization's Violence Prevention Alliance. Again, it is an approach that needs public and political support. This is being achieved by educating communities and not just by locking up 'trouble'. In Glasgow, social exclusion is attacked on all fronts. For the children most at risk there is joint provision with social workers, and for children who are close to being placed in secure accommodation there is smaller, off-site specialist provision.

Reducing exclusion by 87% across the city is the result of great leadership, strong challenge and the commitment of every teacher and school leader to a better system. When you speak to anyone connected with education in Glasgow, the leadership of Maureen McKenna, executive director of education services in the city, is always credited with being the push everyone needed. Maureen recognises that there are no overnight miracles. 'You don't come to work in Glasgow if you are looking for an easy shift,' she tells me. Maureen is not someone who minces her words. She is serious about the mission and clear about the message: 'Understanding where the children have come from. Trauma informed practice. Nurture grown in Scotland. Adverse childhood experiences informed.'

The most powerful, and probably the most challenging, aspect of her leadership is the visibility of exclusion data. Maureen distributes and displays scattergraphs of exclusions and these are laid bare at meetings with head teachers. She has established high expectations for all adults working in schools, even scuffling with the unions early on during the changes. I know myself from working across local authorities that this is not an easy path to tread. Watching head teachers shuffle uncomfortably in their chairs during a meeting is a risky business. The balance between effective challenge and shaming people into a defensive response requires great leadership and a deep resolve. I haven't met Maureen face to face but I suspect she cowers to nobody.

Contrary to popular belief, the city's capacity for supporting children with additional needs has grown, not reduced. The myth that Glasgow 'got rid of their special education provision' is nonsense. Hard decisions were made. Some provision was closed and the money redirected. Some strong alternative provision was enhanced. Some mainstream provision made space for on-site Nurture provision.

Maureen knows why separating children into specialist provision is not the answer. Enhanced Nurture in mainstream schools means that 'when children look out of the window they see other children who are self-regulating, playing and socialising'. Of course, in many schools for excluded children they look out of the window and often see a very different example. That image really stuck with me. It cuts to the heart of why inclusion is so necessary and why we need to be so careful when setting up alternative provision. In the worst cases, the children might be sitting in an almost derelict building looking out of the window at dysregulated kids, and beyond towards the gleaming steel and glass of the new school to which they once belonged.

Delivering high quality training is a key part of the Glasgow Educational Psychology Service which was central to the development of the Nurturing City. In Glasgow, educational psychologists are not working in partnership with teachers; they are in the team and not on the subs bench. Throughout my work across Scotland, I have seen educational psychologists leading the shift in practice. In England, they are given little respect and left to deal with the 'difficult cases'. They are not involved in policy or practice at a local or national level. They don't deliver training or lead initiatives. It is a nasty, ignorant arrogance that dismisses the advice of highly qualified professionals 'because they are not teachers', but it is not uncommon in England. Scotland's example is one that nobody should be too proud to examine and follow. When educational psychologists are trusted and respected they become an essential part of the team.

> Nurture has been a substantial part of a success story in education in the city which can point to a clear reduction in pupil exclusions, an increase in attendance and a dramatic improvement in Glasgow establishments' capacity to hold on to the most vulnerable young people.[1]

Maureen McKenna adds:

> We have doubled the proportion of senior pupils gaining higher qualifications in the same period that we have reduced exclusions. This is not just about inclusion; it is about providing our young people with qualifications which open doors for them – doors which were previously closed.[2]

Exclusion used to spike in Glasgow in November and March, when everyone is creaking towards the end of term and everyone is exhausted. Maureen focused minds on these peaks, as all schools must. Making everyone aware of the risky weeks for exclusion promotes a positive shift in adult behaviour.

Provision embedded into mainstream sites can be flexible and responsive. Children will opt into and out of Nurture. A Nurture revolution across a city sounds expensive but the Glasgow Model has not had money lavished on it. It is a city-wide collaboration using existing funding in a more solution focused way. There has been some additional money for nursery and Nurture corners but this revolution did not result from new money. At the heart of it is collaboration, togetherness, shared values and a willingness to work together to direct the money where it can be most effective.

The next steps for Glasgow are to continue to refine and shape specialist provision as the needs of the children change, to have more practical human resources processes that eliminate abuse of power from the adult, and to develop the conduct, competency and care of all who work with young people.

---

1   Sam March and Maura Kearney, A Psychological Service Contribution to Nurture: Glasgow's Nurturing City. *Emotional and Behavioural Difficulties*, 22(3): 237–247 at 237. Available at: https://www.northayr-edpsychs.co.uk/wp-content/uploads/2018/01/Nurture.pdf.
2   Personal correspondence.

Ian Anderson, head teacher of Bellahouston Academy in the south-west of the city, who I interviewed while researching this book, captures the spirit of the Glasgow Model:

> The Glasgow Model is a reflection of the constitutional debate in Scotland. It is redefining who we are and what we stand for. It speaks of a Scotland that is proud of its care for each other, for social justice, for equity and an international outlook. It isn't about other people's children, it is about everyone's children.

The Glasgow Model is now influencing systemic change in Dublin. Caroline Martin, chief psychologist at the City of Dublin ETB, says: 'Integrating the Psychological Service in the City of Dublin with the school systems is informed by the Glasgow Model. This depth of relationship results in meaningful collaboration that honours local context & knowledge rather than simply imposing "professional expertise" which so often falls short of the mark.'[3]

ON-SITE NURTURE PROVISION

The idea that pupils who have been excluded could remain on site is a difficult one for some teachers. Perhaps there have been a number of unresolved incidents fuelled by poor communication which have caused actual or perceived pain. It is one of the reasons why units for excluded children tend to be in another part of town (the other reason being that it is where the most run-down, abandoned and 'that'll do' schools are located). There are obviously some pupils who cannot be given the opportunity for on-site provision because of safeguarding concerns, so there will always be a need for some off-site specialist provision for exceptional (usually criminal) cases. For instance, a child who has sexually assaulted another could not be accommodated on site for good reasons of safeguarding and protecting the victim's rights.

More and more schools are creating their own internal 'units' in an attempt to provide continuity in the child's education, to keep the connection with the school and to avoid children bailing out of study, often in the year before important exams. Specialist provision on a different

---

3   See https://twitter.com/cdetbchiefpsych?lang=en.

site is expensive and becomes less popular when money is tight. There are opportunities for groups of schools to save money by creating shared on-site internal provision, but it needs to be done properly – and that means the right structures, the right accommodation and, most of all, the right people.

However, I don't see it as an either/or. Let's have some honesty about why we need both good quality external and well-run internal provision. There are children whose lives are so chaotic that they need specialist teachers. They are not in control of the chaos, although they must often, as my friend Jaz Ampaw-Farr says, 'navigate the chaos'. Children with complex and often unimaginable domestic problems need specialist support. Without it they present with all the anger, violence and disregard for safety they can possibly muster. Regardless of the quality of internal provision, mainstream schools are unable to manage the 2%. It takes more resources than they can provide to unwrap all of the issues.

But specialist schools are so much more than a building. Their adults are steeped in experience and create cultures that are flexible enough to deal with everything that is thrown at them. They are battle hardened empaths who find a way to work with the child by any means necessary. A good pupil referral unit or alternative provision is a talent pool of specialist teachers who hold invaluable experience. Attempting to close all the expensive provision and fold it into mainstream schools might look exciting on a spreadsheet (if you are that way inclined), but it looks ugly in reality. The result is the same every time it is tried: the most distressed children end up with nowhere to go. The on-site provision is unable to cope with them and they find themselves allocated with a tutor for two hours a week. Their education ends. I worry that we will soon see glorious PR around internal provision and the money it has saved; meanwhile, we ignore those who have been lost, again.

If you are considering creating your own specialist provision then it matters where it is located on the site and what kind of building it is. Using the tattiest Portakabin or the leakiest room in the bleakest part of the school will send out all the wrong messages. Pupils still need to feel like they are valued, even if their access to the rest of the school is restricted.

Here is a list of best practice that I use with schools that are considering developing their own high quality internal provision for excluded pupils:

- Employ the right people to lead it: calm, consistent and relentlessly ambitious for the children.

- Take time to design an induction process into the provision that is uniform and rigorous, including academic assessments, home visits and gradual integration. Don't ever allow pupils to 'start tomorrow morning' and bypass the induction.

- Accommodate the provision within or adjacent to the main school. Having a separate entrance is useful but – at the right times and with the right supervision – pupils should have access to all the facilities.

- Enable pupils to sustain friendships within the main school by allowing some social inclusion. This may need to be supervised.

- Programme different tracks/pathways/train lines for different groups. Some will be on fixed length programmes and will reintegrate immediately afterward and others will have a phased reintegration. There may be some pupils who won't return to the main school full time.

- Design a curriculum that does not limit achievement. This may involve other teachers coming across to teach certain lessons and/or using online teaching.

- Pursue a positive climate that is relentlessly hopeful and optimistic. The full time staff who run the provision are fundamental here.

- Develop trauma informed, attachment aware and adverse childhood experiences (ACEs) informed responses to behaviour with lots of walk and talk, learning breaks and flexibility – not an environment that seeks to punish further.

- When necessary, the pupils should have access to speech and language therapy, counselling/mental health services, therapeutic support, a social worker, attendance support and offender support.

- Keep the important influence of the main school visible in terms of values, uniform, ambition and community.

- Tight, visible (to all adults) and agreed targets should be used to assess and review progress.

- Coaching and mentoring should be part of a daily approach to drip-feeding improved behaviour.

- Set an adult-to-child ratio of no less than one to eight.

- Don't call it alternative provision – it's a terrible name. Call it Nurture, because it is.

WILLIAMS! LOSING A PUNISHMENT ADDICTION

Visiting a school that has been on the telly is always fascinating. I had been laughing at the children's reaction to one heroic member of staff who always seemed to be the first one to any incident. The cry of 'Williams!' would ring around the students as he approached. They would straighten up, check themselves and immediately cease their foolery. It was a reaction straight out of a cartoon or comic book, with a hint of *Scooby Doo*. The producers clearly loved the children's response to him because they clipped it and played it over and over. Each week, I would look forward to the next instalment of 'Williams!' He was obviously a hero of the school and perversely popular. He held the discipline of the school in his hands. An arbiter of right and wrong. Judge, jury and executioner (of punishment). The kind of saviour that, as a newly qualified teacher struggling to keep control of my class, I desperately wanted. The children would quiver as his voice echoed down the corridors. 'Nobody messes with Williams!'

The strange thing is, one day I was laughing on the sofa with Williams and the next he was giving me a grand tour of the school. I had been messaged by one of his colleagues to see if I would come in and talk to the staff about behaviour. I jumped at the chance. Williams appeared to be an absolute legend – and my nemesis. Could I turn him? I doubted it.

Of course, his TV persona was only a small part of his character. I was immediately surprised to see how kind he was with the children and how warm as a human being. As I learned more about his experience, it became clear that he wasn't just a cartoon character. Williams was a deeply impressive man. A history of professional sport as a player and coach gave him a strong reputation in a rugby league obsessed community. He loved his work and was passionate about the children succeeding, but he was also curious about me and my angle.

We spent the day together. I spoke to all the staff and left him with a copy of *When the Adults Change, Everything Changes*, making sure he knew that he might not enjoy it. He laughed and revealed that he was a bit fed up of the shouty performance and that it was difficult to sustain. He recognised more than anyone that children need firm boundaries but doubted whether it would work with kinder words.

Some weeks later, having inhaled the book and undergone a Damascene conversion, he started changing the way he worked with the children. I returned to discover that 'shouty Williams' had vanished. In his place was a man who would arrive at incidents with unusual calm, the irritation gone from his voice. He got it now and was working on a higher plane. The TV producers gave me the side-eye – they were not enthusiastic about his transformation. Frankly, it lacked the drama and, yes, it would have been more convenient for this to have happened after they had finished filming.

The moment that this shift in practice really began to have an impact on Williams came weeks later when a student came to see him in his office. Clearly, she had been volunteered to represent lots of other students who had concerns: 'Sir, we're worried about you. Have you got cancer?' It transpired that his lack of shouting had been interpreted as illness. They had assumed throat cancer and the rumour had spread around the school. Time for an assembly and an explanation.

BYE-BYE BOOTHS

There is good practice in many removal rooms. Caring adults working calmly with angry and frustrated children who have struggled to follow directions. There is mentoring, coaching and challenge so that children can be returned to learning as soon as possible. There is triage, conversation and careful co-regulating. Then there are removal rooms and isolation rooms where children sit abandoned in punishment booths day after day. Their education is on hold. Often, these are not the children displaying the worst behaviour. They are the children who have irritatingly stretched the lines of tolerance. Sitting in a booth, day after day, staring into space; same faces, same stories, same unmet needs. I met a child who had spent 35 days in an isolation booth in three months. That is not an education; it is more like a custodial sentence.

I have seen it too many times not to speak out: wasted lives, wasted education. We need to Ban the Booths – the punishment booths and the isolation booths where children are given hours/days/weeks of penance. Self-electing to sit in a booth can be a choice; being forced to stay in one is quite different. Can you really call a school outstanding if their behaviour policy is reliant on punishment booths?

When we started the Ban the Booths campaign (www.banthebooths. co.uk) the stories began flooding in. Truly tragic stories. Often, children who had suffered the most appalling tragedies were placed in booths for weeks at a time. Children who were dealing with the death of a parent or a traumatic home move or refugee children with post-traumatic stress disorder – issues that would knock over any adult – and with the ever present threat of exclusion hovering over them. Children stuck in isolation booths because the adults refuse to 'excuse'.

There are some really ugly examples of children being re-traumatised unnecessarily because the school wouldn't listen. I have even had parents contacting me after their head teacher jumped up on TV claiming they had the most caring discipline policy and didn't use booths. The parent explained that both were lies and that his own son, whose mother had died less than a week before, had returned to school only to be placed in a punishment booth by the same head teacher. When the father questioned the punishment, he was told that the school had standards and they were not going to be compromised. Something has gone very wrong when educationalists curate their cohort on the back of families who have no voice.

It wasn't until very recently that I realised Ban the Booths had very similar beginnings to the first campaign opposing corporal punishment in the UK. Ban the Belt started in Scotland in 1976 and was led by two mums, Grace Campbell and Jane Cosans. They weren't prepared to have their children beaten at school and were determined to bring Scottish schools into line with the rights children already had in other European countries.

Grace and Jane fought the same arguments that have been thrown up by Ban the Booths: 'How can we possibly manage behaviour without …?' 'Some children only understand …' 'What about the rights of the other children?' 'It doesn't hurt them – ridiculous to say so.' 'Why on earth are we arguing about the stick/furniture?' The parallels are uncanny. I am sure that we will look back on the use of isolation booths with the same weird fascination as we look back at the many variations of corporal punishment. For me, it was a ruler on the back of the knees which stung until you could douse them in cold water. This was ratcheted up to the cane on the backside if stinging knees didn't remind you of your faults.

The Ban the Belt campaign culminated in a judgement at the European Court of Human Rights in 1982 which ruled that Britain must end corporal punishment in state schools. At the time, a survey of teenagers found that over a two week period more than a third of boys had been subject to corporal punishment in Scotland with a strap called the tawse.[4] Reaching for the harshest punishment available is nothing new.

More often than not, disruptive behaviour is directed at a certain teacher or lesson or a specific group of students. Small incidents can become protracted issues, lessons are missed, gaps in learning begin and resentment between children and adults builds up. Rooms where children are held become increasingly crowded and fractious as the day goes on, as bored long-stayers are mixed with furious new arrivals.

Nobody does any work in rooms like these, usually because the drama of new entrants is much more interesting than the compulsory worksheet from the 1990s. The constant flow of staff into the room is also fascinating for the isolated child. Angry adults delivering grumbling youths, senior leaders with crackling radios, admin staff chasing reports and that beautiful moment when a teacher who is not ready for it is left in charge of the room … It is dull in isolation and the best distraction is rarely the work.

I worry about the number of children with additional needs who are subjected to such a cruel punishment as isolation booths. How many

---

4   Mike Lanchin, *Witness History*, Banning the Belt [radio programme]. BBC World Service (2 February 2018). Available at: https://www.bbc.co.uk/programmes/w3csvtsr.

SEND children are caught up in a no man's land of isolation where nobody's needs are met? What is the geographical, key stage, ethnic and gender breakdown of those in isolation for more than half a day? How many schools rely too heavily on isolation as a sanction? How many schools are using isolation booths to hide the fact that their behaviour policy isn't working? Incredibly, no one knows the answers to these questions as the data is not collected.

In a world living with COVID-19, isolation is now a universal experience. The idea that after a long period of isolation at home, children will return to school and face isolation as a sanction is perverse. Surely, things have changed. And as for the dimensions of the furniture? I feel uncomfortable that fellow professionals think that erecting any form of barrier around a child is acceptable.

A great place to start an internal review of the use of isolation and booths is with the governors or trustees. They should be fully informed of the school's policy and have oversight of the data. Here are some useful questions from head teacher Simon Kidwell from Hartford Manor Primary School to get them started:

- Does your school use isolation as a sanction?
- What do children do to be sent there?
- Could you share contextualised data about which children are isolated?
- Do children with additional needs spend time in isolation?
- Do you have data about the frequency of isolation for individual pupils?
- How long do children spend in isolation?
- What are the conditions of isolation (e.g. booth, room)?
- How do children spend their time in isolation?
- How is the curriculum covered in isolation?
- What is the impact over time?

One of the reasons that the debate around exclusion is so charged is that most head teachers agonise over these decisions and try every which way to make it work for everyone. They are rightly irritated when lumped together with other leaders who would permanently exclude 30 children overnight, call it 'tough love' and be praised for 'saving the other children'. Look for the low excluders rather than just the zero excluding schools.

STOP THAT!

- Threatening children with exclusion or being sent home/to another school/to a special school. Deal with the issue at hand. Leave any discussion about alternative or future pathways to a considered, calm and less emotional time. If class teachers are threatening exclusion, it is a cry for help.

HOW TO LEAD IT

- Be present in and around the Nurture provision. Spend time in there, be optimistic with staff and learners, and let them all feel like they still belong.

- Use your values to answer the really difficult questions that arise when weighing up the consequences of high tariff behaviour incidents.

- Visit the home of every student who is suspended from school.

- Resist the tariff of exclusions. Does a nine-day suspension change behaviour better than a three-day or three-hour removal? Suspend for safety, not to satisfy adult emotions.

NUGGETS

- Use your trustees/school governors/board members. Get them mentoring the students at risk of exclusion as early as possible.

- The end of term is when consistency unravels. Everyone is exhausted, the timetable is often disrupted and children who are safer at school than at home start to become anxious. Exclusions are always more frequent in the last two weeks.

- List your alternatives to exclusion in your behaviour policy. Remove exclusion as a default response.

I am delighted that Paul has made the effort to remain with us but he must accept that there must be no back-sliding.

Paul Dix, school report, age 11

Chapter 7

SCRIPTING REFINED

---

100 days hearing the same words.

100 interventions with the same message.

100 adults with the same calm tone.

In the urgency to develop new approaches, don't miss the most important and simple script of all: *ready, respectful, safe*. It is vital that these three words are used in every interaction about behaviour before moving on to a scripted intervention. Secure the simple consistencies before you attempt the more complicated ones. Do you hear these words when you walk down the corridor? Do they fall from the mouths of every adult? Or are they just a sticky note on a long forgotten training day whiteboard?

Of course, the aim here is not to overhear a thousand negative interactions using ready, respectful, safe. Those conversations need to be held away from an audience. But imagine overhearing a thousand positive affirmations using the rules: 'Kind of you to hold the door – thanks for making it safe for everyone.' 'Love seeing you ready and first in the line, Daniel – spot on.' 'Mrs Davy, this splendid young man has waited so patiently and respectfully for me, even though I know he needs his lunch very badly.' It takes a deliberate shift in adult behaviour to achieve this. It takes time to embed the approach and make it happen every day, but it is critical that everyone keeps referencing the rules. They underline the boundaries every single time. More complex scripts can come later.

A hundred different reference points and a hundred different linguistic riffs from adults when talking about the same behaviour creates a chasm of inconsistency within which the child can avoid responsibility. Improvising your way through an intervention ruins consistency. It separates adults by improvisational ability, divides the team and makes everyone 'playable'.

A head teacher of a school for excluded children had been using ready, respectful, safe with her unwilling scholars for some time. She was relentless with it but wasn't sure if it was having much effect. She had decided to do it alone as an experiment before getting her colleagues to join in. However, as with many changes, the children were deliberately ignoring her and hoping that she might give up and go away. Every time children tumbled out of the middle of a lesson arguing with their teacher, she would reinforce ready, respectful, safe. The children were getting the same message each time they ran into her.

She tells the story of walking past a classroom door about a month after she started using the rules as a child came bounding out, aggrieved at being asked to put pen to paper. As the child almost crashed into her, his attention was immediately taken off the argument with his teacher. 'Oh no!' he exclaimed, 'not the ready, respectful, safe woman,' and ran back into the classroom to pick up pen and paper. 'It was at that moment,' she told me with a smile, 'that I knew it was working!'

Persistence always pays off. Bake the three rules into the language of the school and you will have already come a long way.

SCRIPTS THAT RESIST SHAME – THE LAST COUNTERINTUITIVE

Scripts and mantras use the language in your behaviour policy and the language that is in common use in your school, so you need to remove the worst excesses of the policy first. Weed out the labels, the blame and, most of all, the shame.

Shame is an emotional attack on the child's self-esteem. It is not a proportionate response from an adult; it is a barb.

Lots of people were parented when shame was viewed as an acceptable way to manage and curb behaviour. Standing in the corner wearing a dunce's hat might seem like another country, but we now have sofas of shame, tutting chairs, standing with noses against the wall at playtime, 'non-academic' ties for some and other ties for 'others', sticker reward charts, naughty names on the board, rank order of academic ability charts in reception and children being told to stand up for the rest of the lesson. Children are laughed at for their answer, for their accent, for their colour, for their faith, for their sexual orientation, for their trainers, pencil case or mobile phone. Shame is alive and well in schools which don't actively work to root it out. Shame is the bindweed of school and classroom climate. However, it will be appearing in the behaviour policy of a school near you today.

Often, it is not that we want to shame someone; it is just a default, counter-intuitive response that needs to be guarded against. If every interaction is an improvisation, it is easy to say things that, on reflection, you would have chosen to express another way. Gone unchecked these unintentional turns of phrase become a habit and then a daily act. 'I'm really disappointed in you today.' 'I'm embarrassed by your behaviour.' 'When you behave like that you let everyone down.'

Disappointment, embarrassment, letting everyone down. This looseness of language is where shame creeps in – and shame sticks. It sticks with the child and makes the relationship between adult and child too risky for trust. Shame is also toxic. If you thought that naming and shaming children on the board with clouds, ladders and decaying fruit was the main source of shame, you are mistaken – its tentacles reach much deeper.

Schools try not to shame children for their circumstances and yet it still seeps into the language: pupil premium, free school meals, vulnerable group. Tough love, it seems, is designed to excuse such labels. But shame is not character building. It doesn't toughen anyone up. Schools that openly shame children, build it into their behaviour policy or use it as a means to punish can expect the toxic effects to last a lifetime. Shame experienced as a child can scar your self-esteem, self-image or self-belief. Just talk to anyone about their worst subject at school and a faded wound will quickly reappear in adult life.

Shaming seems like the most disproportionate of punishments, yet it is one that can be delivered under the radar of most behaviour policy and practice. As an adult, it is worth checking yourself for the following:

▪ Are my behaviour strategies based on shaming children?

▪ Do I infer shame when talking to children about their behaviour?

- Do I publicly compare children? When? How?

- What do I do to prevent students feeling shame?

- Do I allow peers to shame each other?

- How would I deal with a parent shaming a child at a parents' evening?

- How do I help children who feel shame about their academic or physical ability?

- Which children in my classes are likely to be dealing with shame?

Some children will have learned shame through their parenting or schooling style and others will have learned it through religion.

Islam tells of two recording angels known as Raqib and Atid: Raqib writes down your good deeds and Atid writes down the bad ones (Quran 50:16–18, 82:10–12). Of course, no human can see them because they are part of the unseen that observes everything. Catholic guilt, barely distinguishable from shame, is present in the act of confession, just as other forms of Christianity use guilt and shame to steer worshippers onto the righteous path. Guilt is closely linked with Judaism and Mormonism, and almost all religions regard guilt and shame as antidotes for poor behaviour.

I once saw a laminated sign in a school cafeteria displaying the photographs of two 12-year-old children alongside the caption: 'Tyese and Kaya DO NOT get an early lunch. Please do not serve them.' Presumably for the crime of pushing in, they had been sentenced to long-term daily shaming. I stole the sign.

Guilt and shame are part of being human, but promoting shame in order to control others is not. Researchers using 'observational measures of children's internal representations of their self-conscious emotions', as well as reports by parents, have linked high levels of 'shame and maladaptive guilt' to depression in preschool children as young as the age of 3.[1]

---

1   Joan Luby, Andy Belden, Jill Sullivan, Robin Hayen, Amber McCadney and Ed Spitznagel, Shame and Guilt in Preschool Depression: Evidence for Elevations in Self-Conscious Emotions in Depression As Early As Age 3, *Journal of Child Psychology and Psychiatry*, 50(9) (2009): 1156–1166. Available at: https://www.ncbi.nlm.nih.gov/pmc/articles/PMC3184301.

Of course, you can also shame someone with too much positive public attention. Wise teachers know who responds best to private and public acknowledgement. The difference is that if you get it wrong it doesn't take as long for the child to recover. I have yet to hear a 30-year-old reflecting on their school experience and complain about being praised too enthusiastically by their teachers. To paraphrase Robert Nesta Marley, one good thing about kindness is that, when it hits you, you feel no pain.

SHAME AND BLAME IN OUR LANGUAGE

The language you use in your behaviour plan will become the common language in your school. Gone unchecked it can encourage discrimination, negative assumptions and a presumption of guilt. It can also throw around labels of false diagnosis. Here are a few terms lifted from behaviour policies I have worked on recently used to describe children who are not able to keep within the rules:

Aggressive

Annoying

Attention-seeking

Awkward

Badly behaved

Challenging

Dangerous

Difficult

Difficult to reach

Threatening

Disadvantaged

Disgraceful

Disordered

Disruptive

EBD (emotional and behavioural difficulties)

Feral

Free school meals

Malicious

Manipulative

Naughty

No empathy

Pupil premium

Unstable

Unwanted

Violent

Volatile

Young offender

None of these labels describes a child accurately. Imagine any of them being applied to you or used in a performance appraisal. We cannot be defined simply by our worst behaviour or unluckiest circumstances. Faced with such terminology from the outset, the culture around behaviour is fixed. It is difficult to break away from it. The strategies that accompany these descriptors are always designed to isolate and weed out the problems rather than encourage a culture of positive recognition. Designed for the 5% and applied to the 95%, it breeds a 'them' and 'us' culture that reaches into every interaction.

A quick audit of the language used in your own policy may reveal similar issues. It may not seem the most urgent task but it is no less important for that. When your newest member of staff reads through the policy and uses it verbatim, are you sure that it is clean of labels, assumptions and guilt by reputation encouragements? If not, you could instead try:

Additional needs	Neglected
Connection seeking	Physical
Crisis	Puzzling
Distressed	Regulated
Dysregulated	Safe/unsafe
In custody	Struggling
Mistakes	Trauma

The right language gives everyone a chance to better interpret and process children's behaviour. It encourages a trauma informed and needs based conversation which, in turn, promotes strategies that are likely to work to change behaviour, not punish it.

THE BEST TWO-MINUTE INTERVENTION THAT ONLY TAKES A MINUTE

There are so many quick conversations about behaviour happening all over schools every day. These are the critical conversations – the ones that are the difference between escalation or getting back to work. Never is the behaviour of the adult more decisive than when the child is not following instructions or their behaviour is wobbling.

Nobody has ever improved a child's outcomes by taking them out of the classroom and pointing out their faults. The chat you have with a pupil to try and reset expectations is often unplanned. However, shaping this conversation effectively means you have the best chance of getting back to teaching with a clear head and the pupil has the best chance of getting back to class ready to learn. Done well, two minutes will seem too long.

The focus of the conversation must be returning to learning. If you start unpicking what has just happened the moment you walk out the door, it will be a longer and less productive chat. This will be difficult at first because the pupil will expect that to be the topic of conversation. 'Me? You asked *me* to step out? Carmel was live streaming whitening her teef on Twitch under the desk and you asked *me* to step out?' However tempting it is to get into this, you don't have the time and the pupil hasn't earned the right to be in charge of the topic.

This moment is a true test of your ability to shift your behaviour to get the best outcome. The high energy, intense and even frenetic atmosphere of the classroom will be in sharp contrast to the quiet calm behind the closed door. Sometimes it helps just to drop your shoulders, breathe and take a moment to acclimatise yourself to the new atmosphere. This may not be the moment for your best 'teacher voice', even though cliché demands that it is. Rather, it is a great moment for humility, curiosity and strong resolve.

Social distancing is your friend here. A distance of two metres will give everyone the space they need. Nobody benefits from being close up, particularly when talking about their own behaviour, virus or no virus. If you are going to be made to look into the mirror, you need to see only yourself, not someone else who could be blamed.

When you get to a space to talk, resist the urge to suddenly find a uniform infringement that must be corrected. There might be a time and a place for that discussion, but don't let it muddy the waters now. Similarly, try not to pick up on physical reactions unless they stop the conversation from happening. Ignore the smirk, the slouch or any of the myriad secondary behaviours that are irrelevant to the present behaviour. Avoid the temptation to recognise repetition: 'This is the third time this week you have chosen to infringe the rules!' or to label or pass judgement: 'It was you. You did it deliberately.'

Here are some suggestions for resetting and returning routine:

- Start with curiosity and a space for the child to speak: 'Are you OK? I thought it would be better to talk away from everything. I was wondering what was up.'

- Accept where we are: 'I asked to speak to you because I noticed you were struggling to keep to our rules.'

- Signal where we are going: 'This is just a pause – I want to get you back in and working.'

- Reset expectations: 'We have agreed that "safe" is one of our rules. I need you to …'

- Offer help: 'What do you need most right now to help you get back to learning?' or just: 'How can I help now?'

- Plan to go back in: 'OK, breathe. We need to "go again".' Or 'When I/we/you go back in, I'm going to make it easy for you to walk back in/move desk/save face.'

Of course, the way you ask a pupil to leave the class or walk away from their group for a chat sets the tone for the rest of the conversation. I have often misjudged this and 'sent out' the child rather than asking them to 'step out'. If the child's irritation or anger is directed at me from the moment we start talking, and I have not acknowledged it, then the pep talk is going to be a real struggle. The principle of keeping your own emotions out of these interventions is worth remembering too. The resetting and returning routine will help, but there is also a moment when the door closes and you look each other in the eye. So much is unspoken yet absolutely clear. The child is reading you as you are trying to read the child. Before you open your mouth, check what you are already saying physically. Drop your shoulders, relax your thumbs and put your hands by your side. If you are prone to lots of gesturing, this may be a good moment to resist.

Some children will need a bit longer to breathe, shake it off and walk back in. Sometimes you will need to return separately to allow the child to save face. These small concessions are important. At first the class will check your emotional state as you resume teaching; after a while, they will realise that you are giving nothing away. How the child returns may affect their ability to stay. You don't want them walking back in and taking a round of applause, and neither do you want the collective 'Oooooo' as they perform the walk of shame. Having a calm, planned and low volume chat attracts far less attention than the traditional 'hairdryer' chastisement that stops everyone working as they tune in to listen.

Setting a new rhythm to these short interventions makes them more predictable, safe and effective. Reducing the number of pupils removed from class, while making sure that everyone stays within the boundaries, is the road to closing the removal room and creating a model of inclusive practice. A little piece of nirvana.

DEVASTATING TONE DROPS AND PERFECT PAUSES

When your pupils know you well, a sudden change in tone can be devastating. 'Aw, don't be like that, Sir,' is an oft repeated phrase. It is a signal that things are going well, that the message is getting through, that relational capital is healthy. Couple that with a tactically assertive turn of phrase and you will be more effective than a raised voice can ever be.

'I need you to focus on this paragraph. I understand Nicky was making faces at you – I will speak to him. In two minutes I am going to come back and check on you, and I will see the first two sentences complete.'

'Awwwwwww, don't be like that.'

'Thanks for listening.'

The impact comes from your inexpressive tone, not from your emotion. The lightness of your usual breezy self should bring this new tone into sharp relief, making it highly effective.

When used well, the pause can communicate brilliantly. When overused, it just becomes 'waiting for children to notice I have stopped talking'. There is a time and a place.

Here are five perfect moments for a pause:

1. When walking out of class to speak to a child about their behaviour.

2. When you have the full attention of the class. The temptation is to leap straight into the silence in case it disintegrates. Learn to hold the moment.

3. When you have been told a lie. It's a good time to stop and rethink.

4. When a child storms out of the room. Breathe!

5. When a child is rude to you (again).

Pauses work when you have the attention of the room. It can be a useful cue for attention or a deliberate prompt for reflection. A pause is completely useless if you are struggling to get everyone to listen. In a chaotic situation, a pause is easily misinterpreted as indecision or weakness.

'I'M BORED WITH THE SCRIPT!'

The 30 second script is a basic intervention that can be easily adapted:

1. I noticed you are … (*Identify the behaviour*)

2. You broke our rule about … (*Connect the behaviour to the rule*)

3. You have chosen to … (*Map out the consequence*)

4. Do you remember last week/yesterday/five minutes ago when you did brilliantly? That is the conduct I need to see from you today. (*Refer back and reframe*)

5. Thank you for listening. (*Walk away and don't look back, then give the child some take-up time*)

Regardless of your dynamic use of shifts in tone and pauses, scripts used in the same way and in the same context will become dull, boring and repetitive to the children. This is not necessarily a bad thing. They weren't designed to be enjoyed; they were designed to keep everything calm and rational. You might choose to adapt the script to make it seem more natural, but the most wily will see through that fast enough. The key is to explain to the children why you are using the script and that it is just a calm response that everyone can trust.

For children who repeatedly find themselves on the receiving end of the script, their irritation with it might be a consequence of them trying to influence your response. I have always found that those who don't like the script get annoyed at how expertly you are holding to your boundaries and simultaneously holding them to account. You should not change your approach simply because a child is upset by it. Every parent knows that being upset is not necessarily a sign that the child has been badly treated; sometimes the child is upset because they cannot step over the boundary that you have held to so beautifully.

You will know when the script is consistent between colleagues when pupils complain that 'Miss Harris said the same thing to me yesterday.' The more the pupils become acclimatised to the 30 second script, the more they will see it as part of the system, rather than just an argument with an individual adult. It ties adults together subtly – almost as if we had planned it.

It worries me that pick-and-mix behaviour systems grab hold of the 30 second script as a technique without first doing the hard work behind it. Even worse, they then use it as part of a zero tolerance regime. After all, from the children's perspective, if the adults cannot be consistent about using the rules in casual interactions, then what chance is there of any consistency when the pressure is really on?

ASSERTIVE REDIRECTION

If the conversation is a redirection rather than a restoration then it can still hold up the mirror successfully. If you are moving from 'just telling off' towards a restorative model, then the following questions might be a useful staging post:

- I need to talk to you about our 'ready, respectful, safe' rule.

- You know the routine for ...

- You could make this right by ...

- Where in the room would you learn best?

- Let's focus on what is going to happen next.

- I don't expect I will need to speak to you again. You look ready to work.

SCRIPTING POSITIVE PHONE CALLS HOME THE PORTOBELLO WAY

Portobello High School in Edinburgh is steeped in relational practice. Head teacher Ruth McKay and deputy Luke McAllister are always looking for refinements that can support all aspects of the relational policy after the adults changed.

Luke told me: 'We noticed that some colleagues were resisting contacting home and were a bit confused. Surely, we thought, everyone knows how to make a phone call.' He went on to explain:

The issue we had is that while the SLT and pupil support leaders make calls home all day long, we were aware that this was not the experience of many of our colleagues, and from our initial feedback it was clear that the idea of making calls home was actually quite uncomfortable for many teachers. We sought to develop staff confidence around calls by creating individual praise call scripts. The language of these scripts was intended to support staff in making quick calls home to deliver some good news and then get out of the conversation.

We then developed staff's individual language into their own credit card sized script to sit behind their ID badge. For most people it sounded a bit like:

- In: 'Do you have one minute for a bit of positive feedback?'/'I'm just about to teach but do you have a second for some good news?'

- Message: The message should always link to our over and above behaviours: achievement, resilience, contribution.

- Out: 'That's it, I just want to pass that on before the weekend – thank you.'/ 'That's my next class heading my way but I just wanted to pass that on.'

To put these scripts into practice we also highlighted learners from our new intake that would benefit from a call within the first day or week – essentially, young people that we knew from transition information were more likely to display distressed behaviours. We adopted the principle of developing a relationship with the parent before we needed it.

For Ruth McKay, changing the culture of the school is something that cannot be left to chance. Although Portobello is a beacon of good practice, Ruth will not sit back on the incredible achievements of her colleagues. She describes the erosion of the culture as if it were a bindweed: 'Unless you hunt down and dig out every last root, old ways will find a way to grow – and before you know it, it starts to suffocate innovation. We continue to be a work in progress. Constantly refreshing training for staff and holding to our core values.'

LETTING GO

Working with a group of head teachers in Egypt on developing new policy around behaviour and relationships, there was real confusion. Like many schools they had a short acronym, MAGIC (which stood for manners, achievement, something, something, creativity), which they found utterly satisfying, neat and tidy (even though it was still difficult to remember!). It may have been the result of a moment of inspiration from an individual or a comprehensive collaborative process over time. It was embedded into every policy, letterhead and classroom poster. Everyone agreed that it was simply marvellous. Everyone apart from me.

The difficulty comes when you try to layer a simple and concise behaviour/relationship policy over the top of the world's best acronym. Three simple rules combined with a list of values encapsulated in 'Go for 5' or 'Resilience Fingers' becomes three rules and five values. Add in a mission statement and ready, respectful, safe is easily lost.

Every time, the same discussion unfolds as I try – very sensitively and without upsetting the people who created it – to remove the acronym from the policy. 'We really like it. Why can't we just use it instead? Really? I mean, we've laminated it.' Sometimes it is hard to let go.

Values are critical for guiding an organisation. Simple rules are critical for guiding large numbers of children. Watching adults in the corridor trying to explain to Riley that kicking the hell out of the glass door doesn't fit with our inspiration value is always amusing but rarely productive. The efficiency of three rules uncluttered by anything else is so important that you might want to shred even the most appealing slogans from the past and start anew.

STOP THAT!

- Trying to script every moment of the school day. Scripts are not there to make micromanaged compliance routines more palatable. They are about getting around some difficult moments, not creating more problems. If the desire for consistency of tolerance (i.e. wanting everyone to respond to behaviour with exactly the same universal punishments) has made everyone parrot endless robotic behaviour commands, then the point of the script has been missed. A 30 second script is there to support and protect. It should never be used to deskill teachers or pretend that 'If I say this script then this magic will happen.'

- The mundane and mechanical deployment of any script will kill the strategy. Scripts need practice and discussion and then more practice.

- Imposing scripts from above doesn't work. Build scripts from classroom experience and involve all adults in creating and agreeing with them.

Don't keep the script (or new versions of the script) from the children. If you explain why adults are using the script, and when they will use it, you can teach them to expect it.

HOW TO LEAD IT

Your script needs to mirror the scripts everyone else is using. In fact, when you go off script it will cause confusion and discourage any colleagues who were dubious about the strategy.

Remind students that adults are using a script to keep everyone calm and safe during the tricky times.

Encourage colleagues to share examples of the script being used to positive effect.

NUGGETS

The best scripts don't sound like a script at all. Learning the words and the process is just the first step. Reaching master level at scripting inevitably means less talking and more physical cues.

If children complain about the scripts, don't deal with it straight away. Instead, find a calm moment to talk them through why you are using it and how it protects everyone.

If you share the scripts with parents, make sure they have access to training on how to use them, so they see scripts as part of a climate around behaviour and not as 'magic words' that can be used in isolation.

He has shown some improvement in the subject but he is prone to moods and fits of whimsy – an unattractive trait.

Paul Dix, school report, age 11

Chapter 8

LEAD LIKE A TORTOISE

Sometimes revolution is better in slow motion.

Leading a school through a change in policy and practice is not a job to be rushed. It requires a great plan, patience and a relentlessness that signals to everyone that you are not changing course. Larger schools, particularly larger secondary schools, can take longer to turn around. Colleagues who have been working in an unsustainable high exclusion environment can naturally struggle with the flip to a relational approach. Sometimes revolution has to take place in slow motion so that everyone feels comfortable with new practice.

The best place to start is always with adult behaviour, with consistency and with positive recognition. Get this right first. Resist the urge to immediately change the system of consequences – they can be changed later – even if there are moments where the two seas meet and it is a bit messy. When new positive practice clashes with the old consequences system, you will know it is time to adjust.

Triage and a less punitive classroom plan can be staging posts from which you can go further, if you choose to do so. They do not require a complicated reorganisation of resources and they still leave the teacher in control of the consequences. If you want to go at a slower pace, you could start with changing what happens when pupils are asked to leave a class. Reframing lesson removal as 'a child needing more support' (than can be reasonably be given while teaching a full class) can slowly shift thinking. Class teachers gradually realise that they don't have to emotionally invest in poor behaviour and a calm consistency grows. At the same time, middle leaders are nudged into action on behaviour ('Hmmm, I think you will find that is a departmental matter') and the triage team quickly become experts at their craft.

However, regardless of how slow and incremental the changes are, some colleagues may struggle with these shifts. They will recognise the values at work and may not share them. At the heart of this conflict is the battle between giving children what they 'deserve' and what they 'need'. Some people's empathy is limited – so unless the action is squared off with a sanction that bites they will never be satisfied, often regardless of the child's context. This is not a reason to retreat. Imagine introducing a full-on micro-controlled punishment regime into your school. I suspect there would be a few people looking at teaching vacancies online with a little more urgency the next morning.

Leading with relationships at the heart of your policy is a steep path initially, but then it opens out into fields of flowering clichés – actual sunlit uplands. As changes in practice become embedded, you may be surprised at how some colleagues will don rose tinted spectacles, often less than a term into the new practice. For some, the system that was failing in front of their eyes takes on a romantic soft focus. 'Man, I miss those pink slips.' 'Life was better without take-up time.' 'I used to quite like supervising the booths.'

It takes time for a new rhythm to settle in a school and for new values to embed. Some people struggle with change regardless of the direction. Some will want to know if you are committed to the new direction, while others will try to test the new policy just to see if it breaks. Of course, most of the team will follow loyally and adapt quickly. Just like the children, there are the 95% and the 5%. Sustaining change means unrelentingly reflecting the success of the 95% of adults and supporting the 5% with all your skill, compassion and expertise.

Whatever the initial outcome of your behaviour revolution, percolating consistent behaviour practice over time will be essential. Seismic shifts in behaviour sometimes happen overnight, but these schools are rare exceptions. More often, change takes time and patience and pain and angst and controversy and cake. The bigger the school, the harder it is to turn the ship. Eighteen months to achieve behaviour nirvana is probably as fast as anyone would want to go. There is less risk and less pressure when you have five terms to bring about change rather than five weeks or, recklessly, five days.

Let's cut to the chase. Here is a quick list of what not to do when introducing new policy and practice – the stuff to avoid, like a deputy head teacher approaching you holding a timetabling spreadsheet or a PE teacher forcing the keys to the minibus into your hand.

Don't:

- Plan any new initiatives for at least a year that would take the focus away from behaviour change (even if it is all going brilliantly).

- Change anything unless the head teacher/principal is on board and in post.

- Try to patch a lack of leadership with behaviour training.

- Change policy without training all of the adults first.

- Remove every consequence for poor behaviour and leave your staff without a life raft.

- Give materials/books/links/resources to the SLT without sharing them with all colleagues.

- Issue new policy or practice guidance without consultation.

- Try to implement everything all at once.

- Overuse scripted interventions by creating one for every situation. One script for the 30 second intervention is enough. When everyone has nailed it, you can then consider one more. However, there is a danger that the technique will become ineffective if it is overused.

- Panic because a small minority of pupils try to test the new system. Expect it to happen and plan for it.

- Imagine that good ideas play out on their own. Change and improvement is hard work: the 'easy' solutions are never easy.

THE BIG SQUEEZE

When the school policy is settled and consistently applied, your work is not done. To reduce higher level sanctions and to continue to develop relational practice, there are pressure points that need to be pressed gently and constantly.

MIDDLE LEADERS

It is critical that middle leaders own and deal with poor behaviour. It stops incidents from escalating and it is the best support for the individual class teacher. At the end of the school day, middle leaders should be resolving incidents within their faculty alongside teachers. A quick review of the triage record and essential conversations to support teaching staff should mean that there are no outstanding issues for teachers to take home with them. This 10 minute round-up means that everyone can truly start the next morning with a clean sheet. In schools where middle leaders evade any responsibility for behaviour, the SLT quickly cop the blame for everything. A divide can quickly grow as everyone asks, 'Who is going to solve our problems?' In schools where middle leaders openly blame senior leaders for behaviour within their faculty, things have got serious and they aren't going to get better any time soon.

LESSON REMOVALS

Supporting, skilling and reskilling classroom teachers reduces lesson removals. There should never be a pressure not to send anyone out – that is self-defeating. But neither should data on lesson removal be published to publicly shame teachers into holding on to distressed children. The answer lies in professional development, coaching and mentoring teachers until they can do the same for others. Maintaining the resources and focus on teacher development is difficult. Many other priorities are waiting in the wings to upstage training in relational practice. A great deal of money is directed at managing children when they are removed from class. Imagine a system where this money was redirected to support teachers proactively, and not just after the event. It is possible to reduce lesson removals to an absolute minimum, but this requires support for teachers, not criticism of them.

EXCLUSION DECISIONS

The procedure for making decisions on exclusions is critical. Left in the hands of one person, it can become a lonely choice and may rely on process more than what is in the best interests of the child. In schools with high rates of fixed-term exclusions, everything becomes reliant on the exclusion process. That is why pressure on reducing exclusions should not come first – you are removing a structural beam that risks bringing the house down.

As the practice becomes more relational, as children are removed less and less from lessons, and as middle leaders adopt a 'buck stops here' approach, there will be fewer children moving towards exclusion. You cannot rely on this alone, however. A weekly review of fixed-term exclusions, including the key voices involved, is essential in schools where suspension or exclusion has become automated, expected and horribly inevitable. The head teacher, special needs coordinator, pastoral deputy and governor/trustee need to have hard conversations about each case and make sure the right decisions are being made on number of days and type of consequence.

TRIAGE FILTERING

A close weekly examination of how triage is filtering pupils is valuable too. Identifying repeat incidents with the same child may be obvious, but there is often more useful information in the data set – for example:

- How soon after the start of the lesson was the pupil removed?
- Did the teacher use take-up time?
- Are pupils being removed for serious breaches or repeated low level disruption?
- Are incidents happening for the same child, in the same lessons, at the same time of week, at the same time of day?

- Is the teacher applying the same consequences each time or are they adjusted to context?
- How long does the pupil take to be calm enough to work in the work room?
- Does the pupil report confusion with the work?

REDEPLOYING RESOURCES

As relationships and behaviour improve in lessons, call-outs become less frequent and triage is almost empty, so staff and resources need to be redeployed. At one secondary school in Oxford, behaviour practice in classrooms improved so rapidly that their removal room was empty. The leadership moved quickly to employ a counsellor and transformed the room into a space where conversations could take place. Removals are now rare and pupils are met with care, compassion and empathy, which returns them back to productive learning better than any punishment could do.

ROUTINES ARE NOT THE ONLY ANSWER

Teaching behaviour is so much more than teaching routines. Of course, routines are important, but they can also become an obsession for some schools and a route towards a lack of tolerance. The search for precision in routines can become a mechanism to root out and remove those who step out of line. Leading a school by micromanaging behaviour routines is deliberately excluding some children from the learning.

There are elements to a behaviour curriculum that need to be taught. This is more than simply recognising emotions or trying to instil resilience. Teaching children about the amygdala response, how trauma affects the brain, how attachment works, how autistic children might have different ways of responding and communicating, how to help a friend with attention deficit hyperactivity disorder and how we can all make small adjustments to help. This curriculum is not something that can be conveyed in a few fleeting moments in a PSHE lesson. 'OK, we've got 10 minutes – we can just run through puberty ... Why isn't my PowerPoint working?' Teach the children the information that we are desperately trying to retrofit into adults, and set aside enough time to teach it – in coaching groups or in form time through explicit modelling. If we stop the cycle of ignorance, the next generation might deal differently with their own children.

Don't leave the children with just the 'what' – give them the 'why' too. A 5-year-old child knows that some of her classmates have additional needs. At what age should children be encouraged to understand this behaviour properly? Should the conditions that affect behaviour be a secret shame until realisation finally comes in adulthood? A behaviour curriculum should not be a hidden curriculum. It should teach about behaviours that reflect individual needs. Sensitively framed and delivered, it can help children to understand each other better and make sure that everyone is looking at behaviour through the same lens.

TRAINING, CULTURE AND CHANGE

Engaging a succession of speakers, most of whom will PowerPoint you into submission, never translates into sustained change. They leave ideas sprinkled like glitter that are swept up and binned at the end of the day. Unless there is an in-house team ready to recycle them into practice, they are just glittery bin juice.

Solely relying on ideas 'in house' also has its dangers. I once went to a school whose retiring head teacher had not allowed trainers or speakers from outside the school to lead training for 15 years. When I arrived they side-eyed me suspiciously. Ten minutes in and minds were being blown with the most seemingly obvious stuff. They had been thirsty in a professional development desert and I brought fizzy chocolate water. I think they were a bit overwhelmed.

Before making major changes in policy or practice, decide what you are looking for in terms of outcomes for pupils, improvements in data and shifts in adult behaviour. Actual changes in practice, testing through action research and selective coaching conversations will drive these outcomes. For whole school metrics, I use 'loss of learning time' as a key indicator. The clock starts when the child has to leave the classroom. Reduce that and behaviour takes less of a toll on achievement.

TRAINING YOUR COLLEAGUES

To sustain and develop the behaviour shifts in your school you need the right people to lead it. Many head teachers would like to think they can be both a visionary leading the revolution and a worker bee on the day-to-day grind. Experience shows that, even with the best of intentions, they don't have either the time or space to do both. There are too many other calls on their time and attention.

Championing new practice needs to be done by people whose own practice is secure. There is nothing worse than having a colleague standing at the front of the room at a training event who, moments before, was bawling out her class so hard that the windows rattled. Look for the calm people, not the ones with their hands up desperate to show everyone 'how I do it'.

It also needs two people to champion the changes, not one. Being a solo revolutionary is not easy and leading in-house training always feels safer as a pair. One of the champions might be a young colleague eager to take on more responsibility, but at least one of them should have the experience to back everything up. The true test of any training is whether the audience believe that those leading it could deal with the pupils in their classroom. If the answer is no, then everything falls apart before it has been built.

Choose the wrong people to lead and things can go wobbly quite quickly. Questions go unanswered, confidence in consistency wanes and lots of adults go back to how they were doing things before. When choosing the right people, it is worth considering those who appear less obvious.

Leadership is about behaviour not talent; not how you were born but how you behave. We think leaders are supposed to be obvious but they are not. You could be the worst player on the team and still be the greatest leader.

SAM WALKER[1]

Training a room (or screen) full of colleagues can induce a cold sweat in even the most experienced of teachers. It isn't easy. They work with you. They see you at your worst and sometimes at your best. They have heard you shout and witnessed you speak in frustration. They may have even seen you at the back of a training day doing an online shopping order and playing a little *Mario Kart*. As you stand before them, you are as full of holes as everyone in the room. This makes things tricky as you seem to have the conch.

Humility is therefore essential. I usually start with a story about how awful I was at managing behaviour when I started teaching. A true story – one the audience can relate to, one that shows I have worn their shoes. Stories connect people. Although endless anecdotes can become dreary, the right story at the right time can pull everyone together.

Here are some other tips that you might find useful:

■ Get the room as right as you can. Adults are often very particular about the temperature – for some it is always too hot, while others close windows surreptitiously. Some don't like too much light. Others can only hear or see from a certain distance or angle. Many don't like to be at the front for fear of being asked a question or to volunteer. A few will try to sit with their back to you, given half a chance, and then there are those who have their favourite spot and cannot concentrate unless they sit there. Sound familiar? Set out the chairs facing the front, give people a choice over where they sit and check that they are comfortable – not too close to the window, not too far from the front. Let them know that there won't be any embarrassing audience participation and no one will be picked on. Pre-empt their anxieties and let everyone in the room feel safe enough to learn.

1   Sam Walker, The Captain Class: A Bold New Theory of Leadership, *The Leadership Podcast* [podcast] (11 December 2019). Available at: https://theleadershippodcast.com/tlp180-sustained-long-term-success-takes-a-different-kind-of-leader.

■ Put out some sweets/raisins/Viscount biscuits (for special occasions) or just feed people. Teaching for eight hours and then arriving at an encingly titled twilight training session means everyone is exhausted from the start. Setting aside a few minutes for everyone to refuel makes a huge difference to how the adults engage and learn (see also hungry children and breakfast clubs). Crap coffee in styrofoam cups with plastic milk and no bickies doesn't convince anyone that you care.

■ Play some music when people enter the room. I am partial to a bit of jungle but this is not always appropriate for all audiences. Apparently, some people don't like dub reggae basslines and percussive loops!

■ If you are using a screen, use PowerPoint as a placeholder for images or video clips. Writing important things on a PowerPoint presentation doesn't make them important or memorable for your audience. If you print out the slides as hand-outs they will make notes and then throw them away almost immediately. Google Docs are your friend here.

■ Never refer to inspectors or use their recent report as a reason for change. Own the change or nobody will connect to it. Lean on your values, not the judgement of those who only come for the day.

■ Capture and share outcomes with agreed deadlines.

■ Think about how people will leave. What do you want them to think about on the way home? The worst thing you can do at the end of a staff training session is to run over time. It leaves people annoyed that you have impacted on picking up their kids/going to the gym/popping a straw in the Prosecco. It is very difficult to get up and walk out of a training session, particularly in the last 10 minutes. Keep to your timings (or finish five minutes early), so everyone can leave relaxed, smiling and looking forward to the next one.

Remember that professional development should come in a regular drip-feed of small bites, not overload. There should be space to think and enough time between sessions to test and ponder.

BEING A TORTOISE AIN'T EASY

I have warned previously about the over-enthusiastic INSET hare who dashes back from a training day to implement everything overnight without a sniff of collaboration. But being a tortoise ain't easy.

Perhaps because of the vigorous multiplying of the INSET hare population, I should mention a new mutation, the book hare, who is more partial to reading books than attending training days. These hares are as speedy and enthusiastic as their cousins. They also have the ability to ruin lots of good ideas by trying to force them on unsuspecting teachers too forcefully and too fast. There are many cases of colleagues being introduced to the ideas in *When the Adults Change, Everything Changes* with: 'We're all going to shake hands with every child from tomorrow,' 'Here are five pages of scripts that you must learn and use from today' and, of course, 'We have abandoned all consequences in favour of restorative questions from 12pm.'

The book hare wants the right things, has the right values and is keen to make change. However, the hare won't wait for others to engage with the theory and practice by slowly digesting the ideas in the book. In their desperation to make things better they often make things worse. There are not two chances to launch new behaviour policy and practice successfully. There is only one.

It is easy to identify the book hare. They read a book, are inspired by the book and then ask someone to come in and train the staff. 'Can't we give everyone a chance to read the book and be as inspired as you were?' I ask. 'But I want to move faster than that!' they say, munching on the tastiest carrot.

When it comes to behaviour improvement, cherry-picking doesn't work. Grabbing hold of enticing new strategies and ideas without shifting the culture and climate is a revolution doomed to fail. The shift in culture and climate comes from adults changing their behaviour and sustaining that change. In order to do that they have to own the changes, not simply have them imposed on their teaching. Being a tortoise may not be easy, but it does mean that everyone experiences a smooth, unstoppable, slow motion revolution with enough time to adjust.

Consistency of tolerance is unachievable, so stop chasing it.

The obsession for every adult to have an absolute consistency of tolerance is misplaced. It is an unachievable goal even in the most ferociously punitive environments. The forbearance of the adult is always affected by what has gone before, by the room, the day, the time of day, the lack of sleep/food/a life, workload and a thousand other factors that influence emotion and response. If you are co-parenting, just think about how differently you measure different behaviours, even after 18 years of parenting, even if both of you are good at managing relationships, behaviour and emotion, and even if one of you is supposed to be a behaviour specialist!

The pursuit of consistency of tolerance is ridiculous and reductive. It doesn't have time for nuance, for reasonable adjustments in the moment or for the subtlety to apply flexible consistency to seemingly inflexible children. It ends up with tariffs, lists of non-negotiables and expectations of behaviour that adults would never apply to themselves. If your school has the words 'failed the room' in its behaviour policy, you are probably further down the rabbit hole than it is sensible to be. Instead, chase an evenness in adult behaviour. A calm, consistent response from every adult. Give colleagues a consistency that is attainable and one that allows relationships to flourish.

IS YOUR POLICY STILL BLOATED?

A single A4 sheet that summarises your behaviour blueprint is not the whole story. The policy that sits behind it also needs a haircut. Even ardent followers of *When the Adults Change, Everything Changes* have presented me with policies that are 20 or 30 pages long or a blueprint that is printed in 8-point font and has every strategy and every technique explained in full.

Once you have established your behaviour blueprint, turn your attention to stripping out the unnecessary blah-blah from your policy so that it mirrors the simplicity of daily practice. In all probability you will need to:

▓ Cut the introduction, particularly the aims and objectives section.

- Weed out the language that carries blame, shame or implicit judgement.

- Beef up recognition so that you have a range of whole school, year group and individual recognition and acknowledgement (e.g. Hot Chocolate Friday, recognition boards, award badges).

- Strip out the last bits of any cumulative or inconsistent rewards system.

- Review lesson removal to include triage and new no-blame processes.

- Shorten the section on consequences so it doesn't look like the biggest or most important aspect of the policy.

- Add a new section about coaching for every student.

- Remove any tariffs that are still lingering.

- Resist the urge to list every possible behaviour that might result in exclusion and instead flesh out your section on early intervention to support students who are struggling.

- Recognise adjustments for children with additional needs, trauma, attachment issues and ACEs.

If you cannot get it down to eight sides of A4 in 14-point font, there is too much filler. A four-page behaviour policy can and will be read immediately or over lunch or at the beginning of a training day. It has a fair chance of actually being a 'live' policy that people use and understand. A document of 10 or 20 pages looks more like a 'file it later' read. It will most likely be filed carefully in that special place.

WHAT DOES IT LOOK LIKE AFTER SIX YEARS?

Fochriw Primary School in Caerphilly has been embedding relational behaviour practice for many years. They were one of the first schools in Wales to adopt the ideas from *When the Adults Change, Everything Changes*. Sharon Pascoe has driven the changes from day one. Six years on, she is still committed to the best relational practice and driving ever higher standards:

> The three rules remain a strong, central feature underpinning everything we do at Fochriw Primary School. They are central to the school's mission statement. These rules have evolved into a pledge, recited by the children, that is shared daily during assembly. A positive change is that the rules are not visible in the school – they are known by heart. They appear only once on the school mural designed by the children.
>
> The meet and greet remains a popular, positive and successful start of our day. This has now progressed from the 'shaky hand gang' to children choosing their greeting – for example, fist bumps, super smile, high five, *bore da* and nod (suggested by the class at the start of the academic year).[2]
>
> A positive change is that with behaviour no longer tracked and monitored, disruptive behaviours are few and far between. The role of behaviour champions is redundant and with calmer behaviour permeating the school, close supervision of behaviours around the site are not a necessity.

Fochriw's adults changed a long time ago and their removal of behaviour tracking and monitoring systems is testament to their development as a staff group.

But let's face it: most behaviour tracking systems were designed to replicate reward and sanction-style behaviour policies. Some were born in zero tolerance environments which are very difficult to retrofit with relational practice. Some colleagues aren't satisfied until they have 'put it on the record,' and the crime sheet against a minority of children begins to build. This approach also encourages teachers to think that someone else can solve everything, and that doesn't work in a culture that values teachers as leaders or one that has relationships at its core.

In the policies I design, there is no reporting of low level behaviour, only arrival at triage and serious breaches and incidents. Recording small

2   Note: this interview was conducted pre-COVID-19.

behaviours that have already been dealt with by the teacher represents unnecessary workload and serves no purpose as the child's behaviour has been corrected and resolved. In many schools, low level recording leaves a digital hangover that is never erased. The tiniest of mistakes and misdemeanours are virtually tattooed on the child. Forgiveness, it seems, is limited in some schools.

CODE BLACK!

Lots of secondary schools use radios for staff who are on the rota for 'on call'. They are summoned to lessons to support a colleague, collect miscreant or intervene like a behaviour superhero. When working in a large urban comprehensive school in the north-west of England, I was surprised to see that instead of one member of staff walking around with a radio there were radios everywhere. Everyone had one and they were switched on, volume up, all the time. Even the NQT in maths had one, although he looked at it with the horror of someone who has just been given a loaded gun.

The disruption the radios caused in the school far outweighed the disruption caused by the children. The anxiety they created polluted the positive climate that everyone so desperately wanted – more Police Academy than Academy. Crackling interference mixed with snippets of broken conversation about parcel deliveries and 'Mrs Short, can you come to the back gate' or 'Have you tried plugging it in?' or 'Um, the police are here – has anyone seen the head?' The students were clearly used to it and most had learned to switch their attention elsewhere. It was irritating but manageable. I sunk into working alongside a child and the noise drifted into the background.

Suddenly there was a loud and clear call-out being shouted across the airwaves: 'CODE BLACK! CODE BLACK!' Code Black? I was immediately on my feet. Code Black didn't sound good and, yes, there were people running. Every member of staff came out of their classrooms and rushed towards a fight that had broken out in the yard at the end of break. But children run faster than most adults, and they had reacted to Code Black like a dog seemingly in deep sleep reacts when his lead is nudged.

There were now hundreds of children pouring out of classrooms and arriving at the fight a long way ahead of the teachers. Obviously, they formed the traditional ring around the combatants, coupled with the essential shouts of 'Fight, fight, fight!' (the world's most uninspiring chant). It took the most determined teachers some time to get through the throng and separate two bedraggled 12-year-olds who were already covering for each other: 'We were just playing.' 'I fell on my own fist.' 'This shirt had blood on it when I bought it.'

Schools can get bogged down in systems that end up not serving the needs of staff or children. Created with the best of intentions, they often have perverse consequences. Taking away the radios from every member of staff changed the atmosphere in the school overnight. Giving earpieces to those who really needed to carry a radio was an easy fix and meant that the dullest conversations didn't need to be overheard. Now when there are incidents, nobody runs and nobody has an audience. Behaviour is dealt with quietly and calmly without broadcasting it.

DRIP, DRIP, DRIP

In the centre of a large English city sits a secondary school. It is surrounded by the worst gun crime and gang activity in Europe in a pocket of raw poverty. The challenges are real. Problems inevitably come into school and staff are rightly nervous about huge changes that might upset everything.

I know the area well and worked down the road. The deputy head aimed to change everything, but he wanted to play a longer game. He started working with just two relatively new members of staff: introducing meet and greet, recognition boards and 30 second scripts. Over time they had created classrooms that were models of the practice. They then worked through the introduction of new routines, shifts in expectation, and creating utterly predictable and safe places to learn. He shared these green shoots with me often. I was impressed with the creativity of his guerrilla-style disruption but slightly frustrated that he wasn't moving further and faster. There were graphs and good data, but from such a small sample of teachers the evidence was limited.

Colleagues started to notice that these classrooms were different, that the behaviour practice had shifted and that the young staff members were succeeding with students who were tricky elsewhere. Their classrooms and this tiny project started to attract others. It was a honey pot of great behaviour practice. Senior colleagues also saw the potential and wanted to move it to scale as fast as possible. But the deputy head resisted. Slow and steady wins the race. Next, he started work on sharing successes with the parents to seed the idea that a new way was possible. Every now and then he would share with me new twists on the ideas, new graphics and new bits of the system he was changing. It was granular and growing organically without big INSETs or revolutionary speeches from the head teacher. There was no 'big sell', just irresistible practice that worked. The best training is often from the teacher next door.

Within two years, every classroom, every teacher and every parent was on board. The data for whole school reduction in excursions and isolation, virtual elimination of detentions and increase in attendance are so good that I use them as examples with other schools. The graphs relate to every child and are on a whole school level. In some of the most deprived and challenging communities, there are schools that shift behaviour practice without recourse to big sticks or mass exclusion. Schools where teachers deal with the most difficult behaviours with the most inclusive and impactful practice. Schools where soft power creates permanent change. There is always another way.

Outstanding schools are not always the best places to learn. They may have moved way beyond behaviour management into the foothills of relationship management, perhaps they are even skipping up the mountain top to behavioural nirvana. It will have taken them a long time to get there and they will certainly know all about sustaining excellence, but the memory of how they moved from chaos to calm may be lost in the mists of time. The school that has just succeeded in this very struggle might well be a better teacher.

LOSING THE TASTE FOR PUNISHMENT RICH

Moving some individuals away from the certainty that sanction heavy behaviour practice offers can be difficult. Colleagues may have grown to rely on the predictable, universal nature of compliance systems. Often, the consequences for the children who don't fit the mould are hidden from them or they feel that they are not responsible for 'those children'. Politicians have a similar blind spot, although for them it is sometimes a deliberate decision; less so for class teachers. Shifting to more inclusive and positive strategies is messier. It requires more nuance, more skill and a more solid base of relational practice.

If you want to remove heavy sanctions from your school, don't start by removing heavy sanctions. It is certainly part of the structure that is holding back relational practice, but, equally, it is part of the structure that many of your teachers need in order to survive. Don't take away the life raft and then try to teach everyone to swim. This risks undermining the changes you are trying to make and forces some colleagues to retrench into the very practice you are trying to help them move away from.

The right place to start is with the most positive steps: the meet and greet, recognition boards and relentless routines. It is always tempting to begin with negative classroom steps or issuing new posters for every classroom. Instead, begin with irresistible practice in which every colleague will see value — practice that will make the use of heavy sanctions rarer than someone in the office giving you a stapler without wanting it back. When colleagues see the strength of renewed and improved consistency, coupled with clear boundaries and positive recognition, the conversation over the use of severe punishment will change.

SYSTEMS LEADERS: GOVERNANCE AND BEHAVIOUR

Governors and trustees are the top of the food chain within any school. They are ultimately responsible for behaviour and yet often struggle to understand how the system works, the philosophy behind it and which questions they can ask to hold the leadership team to account.

Good governance means asking the right questions and not being satisfied with the first answer you are given. Sounds simple, but identifying the right questions to ask is not easy. And neither is challenging teachers who are experts in their field, particularly in front of a board of people who are all experts in theirs. Governance requires team effort and a collaborative mindset, but you also need those brave people who will ask awkward questions and pursue them hard. It is too easy for the data surrounding behaviour to be an afterthought on a couple of spreadsheets at the back of a report, and too easy for people to read the data and just accept it or perhaps assume that they don't understand it. To test the health of school behaviour practice, there are some vital signs worth looking out for.

Data around fixed-term and permanent exclusion are unlikely to fluctuate wildly, so X per term can become normalised. It might not seem worth bringing this up at a governors' meeting, but you should. Neither should governors and trustees wait for a huge spike in the data before digging deeper. There may not be an increase, but that doesn't mean the current data are acceptable. In some contexts, exclusions for minor incidents will go unnoticed by governors, especially when they are presented in a wrapper labelled 'persistent disruption' (which could mean anything). Certain questions should always be asked:

- Does exclusion improve the behaviour of our children?

- Is our exclusion policy trauma informed, attachment aware and ACEs aware?

- What alternatives to exclusion does the school have?

- What is the impact of exclusion on a student?

- How many students with additional needs are being excluded?

- How do these numbers break down by ethnicity?

- Who makes the decision about exclusion?

- What triggers a fixed-term exclusion in our school?

- Are decisions automated as part of a rising hierarchy of sanctions or made individually on a case-by-case basis?

- How does the behaviour policy work to prevent exclusion?

- What is our most successful practice in working with those children/families at risk of exclusion?

- Can we have a presentation from a head of faculty so we can understand the issues in the group from their perspective?

- What is the school's plan to reduce exclusion?

- What do we need to stop doing?

One of the most useful and revealing questions is: Where are the good news stories about this child? Often, governors are presented with the crime sheet and every positive moment is lost in a fog of bad news.

TAKING THE BEHAVIOUR TEMPERATURE

Five ways that governors and trustees can learn more about behaviour:

1. Involve them in whole staff training so they understand the mechanics.

2. Invite them to undertake a 'pupil pursuit' – attending the same lessons with a child for a whole day.

3. Arrange for them to talk about behaviour with different groups – teachers, teaching assistants, pupils and parents.

4. Ask a middle leader to speak to governors about how behaviour works at the departmental/faculty level.

5. Give them permission to stand in the corridors, in the yard or in the cafeteria and just observe pupils and the climate outside of lessons.

When governors have finished asking all the right questions about behaviour, you can turn to the data on physical restraint:

- What level of restraint has been normalised in the organisation?

- Are students with additional needs being restrained?

- How do these numbers break down by ethnicity?

- Who are the staff involved?

- What is their level of training?

- How often is this training updated?

- How do we ensure that staff are still safely using techniques between training sessions?

- What alternatives to restraint are we using?

- Can we see examples of the reports?

- How soon after the incident were the forms completed?

- Which members of staff have been involved in restraints in the past 12 months?

- How are we supporting these colleagues?

- Are formal debriefs undertaken after incidents?

- How are we communicating with parents?

- Can we see an example of a support plan for students who have been restrained?

- How successful have we been in preventing repeat restraints?

- How are we using risk assessment to keep everyone safe?

Your impact as a governor can be huge. You are the check and balance that can make the difference between an ethical behaviour policy and one that rolls over every year without challenge. Make sure behaviour is one of the head teacher's targets for the year. Follow this into the action plan for school improvement and RAG (red, amber, green) rate the milestones with the head regularly to help monitor progress.

Shifts in policy and practice need to be in step with where the organisation is now. The key to leading behaviour is knowing when to stop doing things that may have been successful in the past because the present requires a different response. Schools get stuck with strategies and systems that worked in the chaotic times. They feel a loyalty to the systems and processes that worked in the heat of battle and often fail to recognise that the war is over.

I find myself giving the same advice to many head teachers who are slightly panicked when I suggest that there is excellent behaviour in their school. 'You must have come in on a good day!' they cry, almost disappointed. Despite a good standard of behaviour, the students are still being treated as if every misdemeanour is the start of a riot. Colleagues can also be nervous about shifts in practice. Nobody wants to risk losing control, but without adapting practice as behaviour improves you risk being behind the curve of change. To take advantage of the gains made, you need to change; standing still is more of a risk. Have you ever wondered why they don't use isolation booths in independent schools? Because getting parents to pay for others to be cruel to their children is not as popular as it used to be.

A step change in adult behaviour, a decision not to shout and calmer responses more often, and everything changes. Kindness has its own infectious momentum – but use it. Don't just enjoy it. Don't just revel in the new atmosphere. It is easy to get caught up in the first taste of change and imagine that it will be a cure-all. If only. That adults respond with more kindness is an achievement, but there is no time to relax. You need to use this opportunity to teach new routines and better behaviour.

Kindness isn't weakness. On the contrary, it is relentless, determined and penetrates the grumpiest of school cultures.

STOP THAT!

- Pushing too fast for the change you want or the change you have seen never ends well.

- Asking colleagues to make too many adjustments too soon to their practice.

- Micromanaging change so that collaborative agreements are rejected in favour of performance related targets or, even worse, corporate-style key performance indicators (yuck, need to wash now).

HOW TO LEAD IT

- Do your staff get your first attention for good conduct? Are you using positive cards, spotlighting excellent practice in staff meetings, publicly and privately acknowledging great work from colleagues?

- New policy equals clean sheet. Tear up the old policy. Retrofitting will cause a confusion of theory and practice.

- Don't be limited by technology: digital systems should not dictate. Just because your previous system relied heavily on a certain behaviour software solution, it doesn't mean the new one needs to be designed to fit it. You will end up with a compromise that will translate into inconsistency in practice.

- As a senior leader, you are there to take care of the behaviour of your adults. Those adults are there, in turn, to take care of the behaviour of children. If there is still a line of children waiting outside your office to be 'told off', then that principle is yet to be translated into practice.

- Baseline the opinions of all stakeholders at the start of change. After six months of a new system there will be a small group who yearn for 'the old days'. In their memory, the previous system has become rose-tinted. They have forgotten how they used to feel. How chasing children to complete sanctions had become a full-time job. How parents distanced themselves. How punishment had taken over as the only response. How leadership had become less supportive and more autocratic. If you have the evidence from the original baseline questionnaire, you can gently remind yourself (and everyone else) how far you have come.

NUGGETS

- Swap 'activities week' to the beginning of the year to supercharge relationships and give everyone the time to get to know each other before formal learning begins.

- Put your roadmap on display so that all adults can track the progress and pace of the behaviour work. Rather than hide it in a folder on the shared drive, print it out and post it up in the staffroom.

- Start a CPD reading club and use the prompt questions, think pieces and study notes at www.whentheadultschange.com to read and research together.

Hindered by complacency and lack of attention. Any enthusiasm shown at the beginning of term seems to have disappeared.

Paul Dix school report, age 15

CONCLUSION: REACHING NIRVANA

Great schools are so busy trying to be better that when they reach nirvana they probably don't have much time to reflect on it. Behaviour nirvana comes when learning conversations dominate, when systems and people are kind, when teachers and pupils get heard, and when consistency means every adult is emotionally available.

As the pendulum swings away from the micromanagement of behaviour to a more informed relational approach, punishment rich systems look more and more unreasonable, disproportionate and out of date. These evidence poor, empathy impoverished and ethically skint practices are reductive and redundant. Inclusive, relational and kind schools drive a fairer society. As the adults refine their collaboration, consistency and care, the children – sometimes slowly – adjust their behaviours and expectations. Not an overnight miracle but still magical.

Reaching nirvana means that relationships drive responses and reactions are always proportionate. It means that sanctions have given way to sensible consequences and restorative mending. It means that every child and every teacher has a coach. However, there is no restful endpoint. Sustaining the change in the adults, pupils and culture needs to be worked on every day.

When the insane pursuit of exclusion and strange, unusual punishments reaches its inevitable end, we will look back at the carnage and wonder how we allowed it to happen. There is another way. A more ethical way. A better way for teachers and pupils. Point your classroom, your school and your education system in the right direction, squeeze the consistency between adults, and watch communities and relational practice flourish.

ACKNOWLEDGEMENTS

Thank you to Jaz Ampaw-Farr, John Bryant, Alistair Burnett, Gary Chambers, Elly Chapple, Chris Dyson, Mark Finnis, Simon Flowers, Ollie Frith, Russell Ingleby, Simon Kidwell, Jennifer Knussen, Lucie Lakin, Ruth McKay, Maureen McKenna, Andy Moor, Victoria Musson, Andy Oliver, Peter Overton, Sharon Pascoe, David Shakeshaft, Jon Tait and Darrell Williams.

And every teacher, head teacher, teaching assistant and support professional who has come on-board for the ride. Hold tight …

When you have photographs of your work to share, there is a Gallery of Awesomeness on the When the Adults Change website that is constantly growing. Just email pictures of your blueprints, class recognition boards, positive notes, crazy recognition mechanisms, lanyard reminders, lunchtime recognition displays, Hot Chocolate Friday celebrations and any other innovations you have made using the books as a starting point.

hello@whentheadultschange.com

www.whentheadultschange.com/gallery

Teacher Hug is an online talk radio station for teachers and educators. It brings the best teachers and leaders alongside the most exciting education disruptors to deliver thoroughly thought-provoking content. This is education radio that is buzzing with teaching ideas, workload solutions, education research and the latest in classroom inspiration.

Positive innovation, positive disruption, positive voices.

Listen every weekend and Wednesday night at www.teacherhug.co.uk

ALSO AVAILABLE

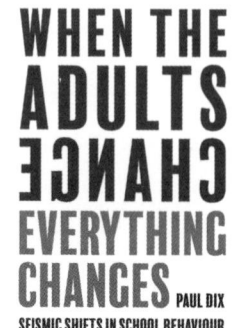

WHEN THE ADULTS CHANGE, EVERYTHING CHANGES – ABRIDGED AUDIOBOOK
SEISMIC SHIFTS IN SCHOOL BEHAVIOUR
WRITTEN AND NARRATED BY PAUL DIX
ISBN 978-178135314-1

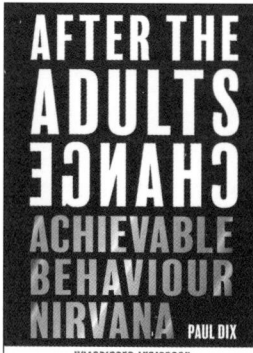

AFTER THE ADULTS CHANGE – UNABRIDGED AUDIOBOOK
ACHIEVABLE BEHAVIOUR NIRVANA
WRITTEN AND NARRATED BY PAUL DIX
ISBN 978-178135396-7

INCLUSIVE, TRANSFORMATIVE AND RIPPLING WITH RESPECT FOR STAFF AND LEARNERS

In these audiobooks, bestselling author Paul Dix talks you through his hugely influential behaviour management approach – an approach whereby expectations and boundaries are exemplified by people, not by a thousand rules that nobody can recall.

SUITABLE FOR TEACHERS AND SCHOOL LEADERS – IN ANY SETTING – WHO ARE LOOKING TO UPGRADE THEIR APPROACH TO SCHOOL BEHAVIOUR

WWW.CROWNHOUSE.CO.UK